behind the song

the stories of 100 great pop & rock classics

MICHAEL HEATLEY
WITH
SPENCER LEIGH

BLANDFORD

A BLANDFORD BOOK

First published in the UK 1998 by Blandford
A Cassell imprint

Cassell plc,
Wellington House
125 Strand
London WC2R 0BB

Distributed in the United States by Sterling
Publishing Co., Inc.,
387 Park Avenue South, New York, NY 10016-8810

A Cataloguing-in-Publication Data entry for this
title is available from the British Library

ISBN 0-7137-2651-2

Designed by Simon Joslin
for Northdown Publishing Ltd, PO Box 49, Bordon,
Hants GU35 0AF

Printed in Great Britain by The Bath Press, Bath

Picture captions
Page 1: Leonard Cohen (left), Neil Sedaka (middle)
and Elton John.

Page 4: Paul McCartney.

Page 6: Neil Young.

Page 8: Buddy Holly (centre) and the Crickets.

Page 9: Chuck Berry.

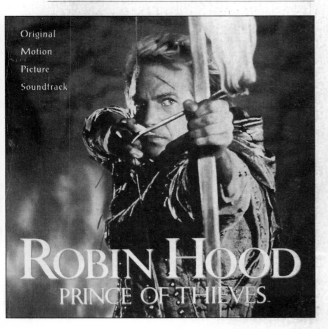

Original
Motion
Picture
Soundtrack

ROBIN HOOD
PRINCE OF THIEVES

BEHIND THE SONG

contents

Michael Heatley would like to thank Dave Ling, Nigel Cross and Graham Betts, experts in hard rock, alternative rock and soul respectively, for their contributions to this book. They brought considerable specialist knowledge to bear and hopefully the entries concerned are the better for them.

He would also like to thank Ian Welch for overseeing the production, Simon Joslin for design, Graham Bateman for encouraging the original idea and Stuart Booth for rescuing the project from oblivion and seeing it had a future.

Spencer Leigh thanks BBC Radio Merseyside for the use of his interview material and also Andrew, Claire and Anna Doble for their help in checking out facts.

Picture Credits
Except where noted, all photographic material comes from the archives of Pictorial Press, London (many thanks to Tony Gale). The photograph of Gerry Marsden is reproduced courtesy of the *Liverpool Daily Post*/Frank Loughlin and the pictures of Ralph McTell and Barry McGuire, which are courtesy of themselves. Acknowledgements to the record companies concerned for single/album sleeves.

hough books about rock stars and groups are relatively common, fewer seem to have been written about the songs they sing. *Behind The Song* is an attempt to redress the balance, its raison d'etre to tell 100 memorable stories behind 100 memorable songs. Some are by well-known acts, others by one-hit wonders who never again troubled the chart compilers. Still others were never hits at all. But all are, we feel, worthy of your attention.

The songs are either of superb musical quality, as with 'Yesterday' and 'Waterloo Sunset', or of considerable social significance like 'God Save The Queen' and 'Cop Killer': sometimes they meet both criteria, as with 'Blowin' In The Wind' and 'Shipbuilding'). And though the songs haven't been selected solely for the stories behind them, it seems that, by their very nature, intriguing songs have intriguing backgrounds.

It was Paul McCartney, no mean writer himself, who once stressed the importance of 'Silly Love Songs' – and although that particular song is too lightweight for this book, he has a point. No matter what year it is, no matter what form the music takes, there will always be silly love songs. Rap songs may not be as affectionate as we might like, but there are still plenty about boy-girl relationships. Our first section thus consists of 25 Love Songs.

All manner of love songs are represented and, indeed, only seven (including 'Oh Pretty Woman' and 'Love Is All Around') actually tell the tale of a happy relationship. There's the unrequited love of 'All I Have To Do Is Dream', the angst of 'Will You Love Me Tomorrow' and plenty of songs about love gone wrong ('You've Lost That Lovin' Feelin'', 'Without You', 'He Thinks He'll Keep Her'). But the times they are a-changin'. Once we thought the coital groans of 'Je T'Aime…Moi Non Plus' were daring: now oral sex in a cinema is discussed matter-of-factly by modern Miss Alanis Morrisette in 'You Oughta Know'.

Flick back three decades to 1967's Summer of Love and you'll find the subject in more universal terms in 'All You Need Is Love' – a surprise product of the Lennon pen, not McCartney's – while the emotional flip-side is well represented by the frustration of '(I Can't Get No) Satisfaction' from Beatles' rivals the Rolling Stones. Many selections in other sections can also be classed as Love Songs ('Layla', 'Tears Of A Clown', 'Creep').

Among the 25 People And Places are songs about political figures ('Biko', 'Happy Birthday', 'Nelson Mandela') and songs about icons (Marilyn Monroe in 'Candle In The Wind'). Don McLean wrote a personal history of rock in the Buddy Holly-inspired 'American Pie', while 'Killing Me Softly With His Song' was written about seeing McLean in concert. Gerry Marsden described the Merseyside he loved in 'Ferry Across The Mersey', but Paul Simon added a somewhat different perspective in 'Homeward Bound' written on a railway platform not too many miles distant.

The communal delights of 1960s rock festivals are celebrated in 'San Francisco (Be Sure To Wear Some Flowers In Your Hair)' and, in the final section, 'Woodstock'. But the decade they graced wasn't all peace and love: the Vietnam war is the background to 'Galveston' and, in an oblique way, to several other songs in the book. Closer to home, the Irish troubles are addressed in different ways in 'Belfast Child' and later, 'Sunday Bloody Sunday'.

Our 25 Rock Classics include records where the performance is often as important as the song. The oldest on our list is 'Crawlin' Kingsnake', but the blues has had a renaissance and John Lee Hooker is as contemporary now as he was in 1949. The Animals, Hooker devotees to a man, showed that white boys really can sing the blues in 'House Of The Rising Sun'. Several songs in this section are allegorical ('A Whiter Shade Of Pale', 'Astral Weeks', 'Mr Tambourine Man', 'Bohemian Rhapsody', 'Stairway To Heaven'), leaving analysts with much to unravel.

The final section centres on Signs Of The Times. Space exploration is dealt with 'Space Oddity' and 'Armstrong', but the songs in this particular category tend to be negative. The vision of a better world in 'Imagine' is a long way off: maybe we are nearer the 'Eve Of Destruction'. The effect of famine was highlighted in Band Aid's 'Do They Know It's Christmas?', while the injustice meted out to political prisoners is the subject of Sting's 'They Dance Alone (Gueca Solo)', a song whose message he drove home by touring under the Amnesty banner. The homelessness of 'Streets Of

London' is more acute today, the subject also touched upon in 'Aqualung' and 'Parklife'. Perhaps it's better to live in 'Hotel California' – although that has as many drawbacks as 'Heartbreak Hotel'.

Teenage unrest has been voiced in many different forms over rock's five decades to date: 'Summertime Blues' (1950s), 'My Generation' (1960s), '1977' (1970s), 'Ghost Town' (1980s) and 'Smells Like Teen Spirit' (1990s) are five examples we cover. Bruce Springsteen wrote about AIDS in 'Streets Of Philadelphia', tying in with an award-winning film. Amazingly, though, the only hit song to have tackled the changes over several decades is Clive Dunn's 'Grandad': maybe it should have been included!

Most of the great performers are featured in *Behind The Song* – Elvis, the Beatles, the Stones, Led Zeppelin and Pink Floyd. The great producers are here – George Martin, Phil Spector. So are the great songwriters – Burt Bacharach, Chuck Berry, Elvis Costello, Bob Dylan, Carole King and Jimmy Webb. Some songs have been derived from existing melodies – 'Blowin' In The Wind', 'Sweet Child O'Mine' and, naturally, 'My Sweet Lord'. Some songs have few words ('Blue Suede Shoes') and some have lots ('Suzanne', 'Bat Out Of Hell'). Great songs can't be defined – if they could, everyone would be writing one tomorrow.

We hope we have included a number of your favourite songs in this book. If not, then hopefully there will be a Volume 2. In any event, feel free to write in to us with your suggestions.

Spencer Leigh and Michael Heatley

Without Elvis Presley, there would have been no white rock'n'roll. And when you consider that 'Heartbreak Hotel', his first US chart-topper, followed orchestral instrumentals by Nelson Riddle and Les Baxter and was succeeded by ballad singer Gogi Grant's 'The Wayward Wind', it becomes apparent that he was breaking new ground. It was his first UK hit, too.

It has been said of his manager Colonel Parker that as time went by he restricted Elvis's choice of repertoire by insisting that the songs he sang should be owned by their publishing company, Hill and Range. It is interesting, then, to note the genesis of this particular song, which was cut on Elvis's first sessions for a new label, RCA Records, who had paid a then astronomical $40,000 to buy out his contract from Sun.

The woman with the original idea for the song certainly had Colonel Parker's ear – she was Mae Boren Axton, mother of future folk star Hoyt and Parker's

heartbreak hotel

elvis presley

public relations person in Florida. She told Parker's new protégé 'You need a million-seller – and I'm going to write it for you.' And that, with the help of Tommy Durden, is what she did. Somewhere along the line Elvis took a share of the three-way credit that ended up on the label, but it's possible the Colonel may have had a hand in that: the extent of Presley's input is unclear.

What is known is that the song had its roots in reality – and it was Durden who had come up with a newspaper story about a suicide victim who had left a note about 'I walk a lonely street'. Mae took the metaphor one stage further by locating the hotel of the title at the end of the street, and that proved the key to inspiration, the pair committing the song to tape in 22 minutes flat.

Mae Axton called Elvis and arranged a rendezvous in Nashville. He was fascinated that her prediction had come true, and asked for the tape to be replayed ten times until he had memorized the lyric and arrangement. From there, it was a short step to the RCA studios to cut the song on 10 January 1956. Producer Steve Sholes was taking no chances on losing any of the Presley magic that had turned his Sun label releases into country hits, and had assembled the usual instrumental crew of guitarist Scotty Moore, bassist Bill Black and drummer D.J. Fontana, augmenting them with a pianist (Floyd Cramer) and an additional guitarist (the legendary Chet Atkins).

The song, complete with its influential use of echo, was rush-released on 27 January, barely a fortnight after recording, and would be featured three times over the next two months as Elvis became a regular guest on the *Dorsey Brothers' Stage Show*. Such exposure on nationwide television took the record to the top of the *Billboard* listings on 21 April, and there it stayed for an amazing eight weeks, selling over two million copies. In the UK it went to Number 2 in the *New Musical Express* charts, one place lower in the *Record Mirror*, and was Elvis's first hit there.

Although Elvis checked out for good in 1977, there are few of us who cannot empathize with this great song.

First released:	1956
Highest UK chart position:	**2**
Highest US chart position:	**1**

love songs

To hit Number 1 with your first chart entry takes some doing – but the Crickets, fronted by the legendary Buddy Holly, managed just that on both sides of the Atlantic with a song that would directly inspire the Beatles and was one of the first songs John Lennon ever learned to play. Ironically, though, this was a song that became a hit only after it was given a second chance.

The title was a direct lift from a classic 1956 Hollywood movie, *The Searchers*. While the film's title inspired a Merseybeat four-piece in the following decade, Holly – who would share the songwriting credit with Crickets' drummer Jerry Allison and producer Norman Petty – had taken the words out of John Wayne's mouth! The Duke was playing the part of Ethan Edwards, a former Confederate soldier, in John Ford's cowboy epic. Little did he know his catch-phrase would soon be a worldwide hit.

Holly's first recording of the song on 22 July 1956 had not met with the approval of Decca Records, the company with which he had signed as a solo artist. But he kept faith in his creation and, when his deal with Decca expired in early 1957, took it with him to Norman Petty 's studio in Clovis, New Mexico.

Petty liked the song and cut it with Holly and the Crickets on 25 February. The intention was to sign with the Roulette label, whose artist Buddy Knox had already scored with the Petty-produced 'Party Doll', a Holly favourite. But they agreed with Decca, as did Atlantic, RCA and Columbia. Only Coral Records executive Bob Thiele heard any promise in the song and signed the group. Because Decca had paid for the first recording, the remake was the one that made it to disc, and was released by Coral – ironically owned by Decca – as the Crickets, not Buddy Holly. 'They kicked us out the front door,' Holly chortled later, 'so we went in the back door!'

that'll be the day

crickets

The reverberations of the record extended worldwide, and in August 1958 Merseyside teenagers John Lennon, Paul McCartney and George Harrison – at that point members of a skiffle group known as the Quarry Men – paid 17s 6d (87$\frac{1}{2}$ pence) to record a version of the song in a studio in the Kensington area of Liverpool, along with McCartney and Harrison's self-penned 'In Spite Of All The Danger'. When the trio became the Beatles, their new name was another homage to the group which had so inspired them. The song also named a 1974 film which starred David Essex, Ringo Starr and Keith Moon, but that was an altogether less memorable affair.

'That'll be the day when I die' has an echo in 'The day the music died', the theme of 'American Pie', which emulated its inspiration by topping the US chart in 1972. 'Holly was a symbol of something deeper than the music he made,' said singer Don McLean. 'The sort of group he created, the interaction between the lead singer and the three men backing him up was the perfect metaphor of the music of the 1960s.' Lennon would doubtless agree…

First released:	1957
Highest UK chart position:	1
Highest US chart position:	1

all i have to do is dream

everly brothers

The transatlantic chart-topping success of this song was no surprise either to the team of Don and Phil Everly or to the husband and wife, Felice and Boudleaux Bryant, behind so many of their hits. The combination had already hit the top late in 1957 with 'Wake Up Little Susie', but it is this yearning song of love (written by Boudleaux alone) rather than the bouncy, teen-style whimsy of 'Susie' that is best remembered.

The Bryants' prolific pairing had started after their marriage in 1945 and hit gold in 1956, when Elvis Presley – then the hottest artist around – had selected 'How's The World Treating You?', a country ballad intended for Eddy Arnold and co-written by Boudleaux and guitar legend Chet Atkins, as an album track. This opened the Bryants' eyes to a new, young and lucrative teenage audience for their songs, and many artists would later cover their compositions. But 'Dream', rattled off in just 15 minutes, remains the masterpiece.

The B-side of the single, 'Claudette', gained much airplay, reaching Number 30 Stateside in its own right, and introduced the public to the songwriting talents of Roy Orbison, who penned it about his wife. In terms of the Bryants' partnership, Boudleaux, a classically trained string player who had worked with the Atlanta Philharmonic, usually dealt with the music, with ex-elevator operator Felice adding a lift to the lyrics.

When the Everlys went for broke and took the big bucks offered by Warner Brothers, they also switched their publishing away from the Nashville-based Acuff-Rose company. 'We needed more freedom,' they later commented, 'but one of the sad consequences of splitting with Wesley [Rose] was that we were no longer able to get Boudleaux's songs.' Those songs, some 750 in total, are reckoned to have sold over 300 million records in the hands of 400-plus artists.

The fact was that the brothers had become adept at pastiching the Bryants' style themselves. There was also the undeniable fact that the twin influences of Brill Building and Motown were about to pen songs far closer to the hopes and aspirations of 1960s kids than the middle-aged Bryants could hope to. It would be the likes of Bob Luman, Sonny James and Chet Atkins, all established artists for an adult market who called on the Bryants' talents in the coming years. The Everlys came back too, in 1972, for 'Rocky Top', while the Bryants were elected to the Songwriters' Hall of Fame in 1986.

Since Don and Phil's definitive version, 'All I Have To Do Is Dream' has charted in the US for different artists in each succeeding decade, from the 1960s through to the 1980s. Singing actor Richard Chamberlain scored solo in 1963, while the subsequent versions have been lovey-dovey duets between Glen Campbell and Bobbie Gentry (1970) and Andy Gibb and Victoria Principal (1981). The sequence may or may not be maintained before the millennium. The seven weeks the record spent on top of the UK chart was surpassed only by Perry Como in 1958.

No less a personage than Bob Dylan acclaimed the Everlys as 'The guys who started it all... we owe them everything.' While Don and Phil were flattered at such recognition, they would doubtless acknowledge their debt to another prolific double act that had supplied the ammunition for their harmonious hitmaking.

First released:	1958
Highest UK chart position:	1
Highest US chart position:	1

will you love me tomorrow

shirelles

Few, if any, would dispute the inclusion of the Shirelles' 'Will You Love Me Tomorrow' in this book. The record is a classic, easily the best record made by any of the famed New York girl groups. It has the catchiest of melodies, a sympathetic arrangement and a sensitive lead vocal from Shirley Alston Reeves, known at the time as Shirley Owens. It was a brill song from the Brill Building where, as the film *Grace Of My Heart* shows, young composers in tiny cubicles wrote hits for the new teen market. One husband-and-wife team was Carole King and Gerry Goffin, and their first song of real significance was 'Will You Love Me Tomorrow'. Their employer, Don Kirshner, gave the song to A&R man Mitch Miller at Columbia Records. He turned it down, so it went to the smaller Scepter label.

A song about virginity was daring in 1960, even more so when the girl is going to say 'yes' as soon as the record ends. Hundreds of performers have recorded the song, although it is strange that so many men have done so – if ever there was a woman's song, this is it. Outside of the Shirelles, the most poignant interpretation comes from its composer, Carole King, who, when including it on her 1971 'Tapestry' album, slowed the tempo and turned it into a plea to save a broken marriage. Dionne Warwick, in a later version produced by Luther Vandross, used the Shirelles as backing singers.

The Shirelles had already had US hits with 'Tonight's The Night' and 'Dedicated To The One I Love' and, as Shirley Alston Reeves remembers, 'When I first heard the song, I didn't think it was right for the Shirelles. Carole King did it more on the country side as it was very laid-back on the piano. There was nothing wrong with the way she was singing it but we were more into R&B than pop. Our producer, Luther Dixon, said, "Just do it as a favour to me." As soon as I went to the session and heard the music, the song came to life for me and I thought it was beautiful. I was crying on that session. It was a beautiful song and the record company knew it was risqué. It was all about, "Will you respect me in the morning?"'

Charlie Gillett notes in his book *The Sound Of The City*, 'Occasionally Shirley's voice sounded off-key when she went up for a note she could not reach, but at its most effective (all the way through "Will You Love Me Tomorrow") the failure enhanced her plaintive appeal. Gospel-based call-and-response harmonies gave the sound an exciting quality which was novel to those who had never been in a black church.' 'Will You Love Me Tomorrow' was the first record by a girl group to top the US charts, and its combination of R&B harmonies and strings brought to mind the Drifters' 'There Goes My Baby'. Carole King, who did the arrangement, was not happy with the percussionist and played the kettle drum herself.

In terms of chart positions, the Shirelles were a moment's pleasure in the UK but a lasting treasure in the States. They had chart-toppers with 'Will You Love Me Tomorrow' and 'Soldier Boy' and cut several other hits, which were often revived by British beat groups. The Beatles recorded the B-side of 'Will You Love Me Tomorrow', 'Boys', which again is a girl's song.

And 'Will You Love Me Tomorrow' lost Shirley her credibility. 'Every time we didn't want to do a song, they said, "What about 'Will You Love Me Tomorrow'?", and we had to do it.'

First released:	1960
Highest UK chart position:	4
Highest US chart position:	1

crazy

patsy cline

For many people, the story of Patsy Cline begins and ends with this song. The former child star turned country diva scored her biggest pop hit with 'Crazy' in 1961, but was dead a mere two years later. Its one-take vocal is still her best-remembered performance. For Willie Nelson, the man who wrote it, it was long-awaited proof that he had a career in professional music, having tried everything from encyclopedia selling to hawking vacuum cleaners door-to-door. Not that he was anything if not cautious: indeed, despite this success and another pop smash, 'Hello Walls', for Faron Young, he remained fully employed as bass player for Ray Price's Cherokee Cowboys before eventually coming off the road to record his own material.

Yet the more successful Nelson became, the more his marriage to wife Martha was put under pressure. Their daughter Lana recalls hearing the news of Cline's air-crash death, and her mother saying 'You know, if there's one woman in the world I hated it's Patsy Cline.' 'I thought it was kind of cruel,' Lana admits, 'but…'

Nelson, who would challenge country conventions in the 1980s as one of the Outlaws, was already having problems with the Establishment. 'If a song had more than three chords in it, there was a good chance it wouldn't ever be called country. And there was no way you could make a record that wasn't called country in Nashville at that time. I had problems immediately because "Crazy" had four or five chords in it. Not that it's real complicated, it just isn't your basic hillbilly song. I could have retired modestly at the age of 30 off the royalties from songs like "Crazy"… but I enjoyed music too much to consider retiring to the life of a writer.'

As he was hitting the road, poor Patsy Cline met her end travelling back to Nashville from a Kansas benefit gig. Ironically, she had recorded the song while on crutches, having suffered a fractured hip and near-fatal head injuries after being thrown through the windscreen of a car. 'Crazy's crossover success at Number 9 in the US pop chart gave her what was to be her biggest hit and the one for which she remains known. The number of 'Karaoke Clines' who have since donned fringed buckskin to yodel her signature tune are legion.

Willie Nelson still sings the song, but to most of us it's entwined with the Cline legacy. Dolores O'Riordan, future lead singer with the Cranberries, had Cline's 'Crazy' 'down to a tee by the time I was six', while Canadian New Country starlet k.d. lang sought out Cline's long-retired producer Owen Bradley to get the same lush, orchestrated sound. She also named her backing band, the Reclines, after her role model.

Amazingly, 'Crazy' has never topped the *Billboard* country chart in other hands (Kenny Rogers' 1985 hit merely shared the title). Even so, it reached Number 14 in the UK chart in 1991 after being revived for a TV commercial, and was twice honoured the following year. The 34th Grammy Awards saw it inducted into the NARAS (National Academy of Recording Arts and Sciences) Hall of Fame, while in September 1992 readers of *Country America* magazine voted it their fourth most popular song of all time.

First released:	1961
Highest UK chart position:	14
Highest US chart position:	9

Roy Orbison's wife Claudette had already inspired him to write a hit song – but if she had been his inspiration then, he took advantage of her absence to pen his second-ever US chart-topper. 'Oh Pretty Woman' hit the top in the UK, too, confirming that the bespectacled Roy was immune to the beat revolution that had consigned most solo artists to a sudden and dramatic demise.

Songwriting partner Bill Dees (with whom he wrote the UK chart-topping 'It's Over') had come round for a session. 'We'd just begun around six in the evening,' Orbison recalled, 'and about that time my wife came in and wanted to go to town to get something. I said "Do you have any money… ".'

'A pretty woman never needs any money,' quipped Dees – and by the time Claudette returned some 40 minutes later, the pair had fashioned a money-spinner that would finance any number of future sprees. Its success would also inspire Bill Dees to walk into the office of the Henderson Construction & Supply company where he had been employed and announce 'I quit!'

oh pretty woman

roy orbison

In the song's earliest incarnation, Roy recalls he 'started playing the guitar and Bill was slapping the table for drums.' But the studio backbeat was supplied by twin drummers Paul Garrison and Boots Randolph. It was the former who claimed to have come up with the socking bass drum sound, taking advantage of Orbison's unusual (for the time) attitude of coming into the studio with no fixed arrangements. Jerry Kennedy, the lead guitarist also used on 'It's Over', came up with the cocky eight-note riff.

Roy's vocals contained a fair share of improvisation, too. 'I was known around the studio for saying "Mercy",' he recalled. 'And when we got to a note that wasn't in my range I substituted the word and everyone just smiled. That's the way we got the growls too. It was a

matter of doing it and waiting to see if anyone said no. This time they left them in.' He also noted that this had an interesting effect on foreign audiences. 'In French, "Mercy" sounds like I'm saying "thank you".'

Worldwide sales of a song Chet Atkins called the 'best commercial record I ever heard' exceeded seven million. It was a song that, in Orbison's words, went through a lot of emotions. 'I didn't think of this as if we were writing the song but the guy's observing the girl, and he hits on her real cool and macho. Then he gets worried, and gets to pleading, and then he says "Okay, forget it, I'm still cool." Then in the end she comes back to him and he turns into the guy he really is... '

It's doubtful if heavy metal hopefuls Van Halen had all this in mind when they assaulted the song in 1982 and reached the US Top 20. Other artists to have covered the song include Al Green, Ricky Van Shelton and the Ventures.

Sadly, Roy and Claudette Orbison, the song's inspiration, would drift further apart and divorce in 1965. Nevertheless, her death in a motorcycle accident the following year devastated the man, and would be followed by the loss of two sons in a house fire. He remarried in 1969, and it was this second Pretty Woman, Barbara, who was controlling his career when he died of a heart attack in 1988. The song was also used two years later in the eponymous film starring Julia Roberts – and, while many contemporary artists were featured, only the original version of this song would do.

First released:	1964
Highest UK chart position:	1
Highest US chart position:	1

love songs

The most covered song of all time – over 2,500 versions, according to the *Guinness Book Of Records* – it is also well known that 'Yesterday' started out with the working title 'Scrambled Eggs'. 'I just fell out of bed and it was there,' McCartney later recalled. 'I have a piano by the side of my bed and just got up and played the chords.' So familiar did the tune seem that he spent the next fortnight asking people to identify it, convinced he had subconsciously heard it somewhere! 'I thought what key's this thing in, and it found its way to a G. I thought it can't just have come to me in a dream. It's like handing things in to the police – if no one's claimed it after two weeks I'll have it!'

yesterday

beatles

Despite the Lennon-McCartney credit, this was a solo effort both in composition and execution. Producer George Martin, who first heard the song while staying with the band at the George V Hotel in Paris before it had acquired a serious title, had made the decision that the song didn't suit the two guitars, bass and drums format – and, when McCartney objected, pointed out that they could go back and re-cut it if his idea of guitar and string section didn't work. Needless to say, the 'fifth Beatle' was right...

So familiar is the song that everyone assumes it was a hit worldwide. This wasn't the case: it became the group's tenth chart-topper in the US, but would not appear as a single in the UK (where Marianne Faithfull and Matt Monro had already charted with it in the year of issue) until 1976. In the States it was left off the soundtrack album to the Beatles' second film, *Help*, and released in its own right.

The song could well have been sung by another singer: it's not widely known that Paul offered it to blues shouter Chris Farlowe, whose biggest hit, 'Out Of Time', emerged from the rival Rolling Stones camp. He also offered it to Billy J. Kramer when his fellow Liverpudlian approached him in Blackpool for a suitable song to record. Paul played him 'Yesterday' and was told it wasn't what he was looking for! It hasn't done badly for a song that its composer – who rates it 'the most complete song I've ever written' – couldn't even give away...

John Lennon hated 'Yesterday', not least because of its mawkish sentimentality. The fact that it was the first-ever Paul McCartney solo track probably didn't help. He used his 1971 album 'Imagine' to have a pop at his erstwhile songwriting partner in the barbed 'How Do You Sleep', snarling, 'The only thing you done was Yesterday/And since you're gone you're just Another Day'. McCartney himself remembers George Martin saying: 'Blimey, he's always talking about "Yesterday", you'd think he was Beethoven or something.'

For its writer, it has been less an albatross than a meal ticket – a fact he acknowledged by reprising it in his 1984 film *Give My Regards To Broad Street*.

Ironically, as with all his early pre-Apple compositions published by Northern Songs, McCartney doesn't own the publishing rights to the song, so had to ask permission to include it. Northern Songs was later sold to his friend Michael Jackson… but that's another story!

First released:	1965
Highest UK chart position:	8
Highest US chart position:	1

breaking up is hard to do

neil sedaka

Neil Sedaka's first US chart-topper from 1962, 'Breaking Up Is Hard To Do', is a classic song in anyone's language. It has since become the traditional set-closer for the American singer-songwriter: indeed, it's doubtful if his dedicated fans would let him leave the stage without playing it!

Born in Brooklyn in 1939, Sedaka was soon to become a classical piano prodigy – but a chance meeting with near-neighbour Howard Greenfield diverted him towards forming a pop partnership that was to last two decades. The duo wrote hits for others as part of the famed Brill Building song factory, but Sedaka craved his own share of the spotlight and hit the US Top 10 in 1959 with 'Oh Carol', a jokey love song dedicated to fellow songwriter Carole King.

'Breaking Up' was initially a title Sedaka presented to his lyricist in the hope of inspiring him. Greenfield was unimpressed, but responded better a second time. The music Sedaka had in mind was inspired by the Showmen's 'It Will Stand', an early anthem to the power of rock. But despite his clear idea of what he wanted to achieve, the song still lacked a key ingredient…until Sedaka came up with the unique vocal hook.

Inspiration came as he lay in bed the night before the recording session they had booked to cut the song. And if arranger Allan Lorber was startled to receive a half-past midnight phone call, then he must have been gobsmacked to hear a familiar voice crooning 'come-a come-a down, dooby-doo down down' into his ear. Anything that could keep him awake had to have *something*, Neil reasoned – and he was rewarded by his biggest hit to date.

Released in the summer of 1962, the song was the first of three US chart-toppers Neil would register. The third, 1975's 'Bad Blood', would be followed by another version of 'Breaking Up', this time slowed down and delivered as a heartfelt ballad. In taking this to Number 8, Neil

Sedaka created *Billboard* chart history in becoming the first original artist to re-record a Number 1 and take it back to the Top 10. Its new, slowed-down and infinitely more thoughtful version was very much in the confessional singer-songwriter mould that had been so profitably created by former Brill Building colleague Carole King.

Before that, though, it had been covered in 1972 by TV stars the Partridge Family, whose David Cassidy elected to stay true to the original teen style. Not that Sedaka was complaining: aside from the royalties, the Captain and Tennille were continuing the tradition and taking 'Love Will Keep Us Together' to US Number 1, again in 1975.

Sedaka himself would carry on singing into the 1990s, remaining especially popular in the UK, and would even take a leaf out of the Captain and Tennille's book by linking with vocalist daughter Dara for a hit with 'Should've Never Let You Go'. Yet, although his latest album in 1996 had him putting contemporary lyrics to classical themes, 'Breaking Up Is Hard To Do' – a classic from his own pen – remained a key song in his repertoire.

First released:	1962
Highest UK chart position:	7
Highest US chart position:	1

you've lost that lovin' feelin'

righteous brothers

Phil Spector's production masterpiece for Bill Medley and Bobby Hatfield, collectively known as the Righteous Brothers, has had more comebacks than almost any record you can think of, with the ironic exception of the Brothers' 'Unchained Melody'. It has been reissued in the UK three times, the first at the behest of Jonathan King when he became personal assistant to Decca Records head honcho Sir Edward Lewis. It is also producer Mickie Most's favourite record of all time.

So, if this is a song with friends in high places, its genesis was almost by chance. The Brothers had performed in 1964 on the same bill as the Ronettes, Spector protégées who featured Mrs S, Veronica Bennett, as lead singer, after which he signed them up.

The three-handed songwriting team responsible for 'Lovin' Feelin'' consisted of Spector plus the husband-and-wife pairing of Barry Mann and Cynthia Weil – themselves responsible for such classics as 'Uptown', 'We Gotta Get Out Of This Place' and 'On Broadway'. Having bought out the Brothers from their contract with the tiny Moonglow Records, Spector had asked the team to write a song specifically for his new act to sing. They flew out to California, spun the duo's previous hits and, ensconced in a Sunset Strip hotel with a rented piano, decided a ballad would be a change of pace to the dance-craze likes of 'Little Latin Lupe Lu'.

Unbelievably, the key phrase 'You've lost that lovin' feelin'' was a placeholder for the finished lyric, but Spector was so impressed that he insisted it be kept. The trio then decamped to the producer's house, where the three together fashioned the 'I'll get down on my knees for you' bridge to the last chorus. It's been suggested that the model for the song was the Four Tops' 'Baby I Need Your Loving'.

The song took ten hours to record – a marathon in 1960s terms, if nothing special today. It also ran for four minutes, in order to take in the anguished coda which so many people associate with the song. But since Mickie Most had blasted the two-and-a-half minute barrier the previous year with the Animals' 'House Of The Rising Sun', radio had been far more receptive to the idea of treating songs on their own merits.

Barry Mann was taken aback, however, when he heard the opening from Bill Medley, the deeper-voiced half of the Brothers Righteous. For a second, he thought Spector was playing it at the wrong speed. In his defence, though, he was soon back in New York at the other end of the telephone. And he wasn't the only one to like – eventually – what he heard. It shot up the charts on either side of the Atlantic, to take top place in both within the space of two days in February 1965.

Jonathan King's patronage not only gave the record a new lease of life, returning it to the UK Top 10 in 1969, but also started the craze for reissuing classic material that would revolutionize the attitude of the music business to back catalogue. The song would also enjoy US hit covers from Dionne Warwick (1969) and Hall and Oates (1980). In the UK, Cilla Black took it to Number 2 later in the year of issue, while TV 'tec Telly Savalas of *Kojak* fame used it to follow up his chart-topping 'If' in 1975 – although his half-singing, half-speaking style did the song few favours, as its chart position (46 places lower) showed.

First released:	1965
Highest UK chart position:	1
Highest US chart position:	1

(i can't get no)
satisfaction
rolling stones

If 'Satisfaction' had ended before Mick Jagger had sung a note, it would still have been a great record. A short one, admittedly, but a great one. It opens with a explosive rock'n'roll riff every bit the equal of 'Bo Diddley', 'La Bamba' and 'Louie Louie'. It continues throughout the record and you become hooked to the rhythm, which makes 'Satisfaction' the perfect party record.

It had come about in a strange way. The Rolling Stones were touring non-stop, and early in 1965 they were in America. Some days had been set aside for recording at the Chess Studios in Chicago – the home of Chuck Berry, Muddy Waters and Bo Diddley – and at RCA in Hollywood. They were to make the album which would become 'Out Of Our Heads' and their record producer and manager, Andrew Oldham, wanted Mick and Keith Richards to write a Motown-styled song similar to Marvin Gaye's 'Can I Get A Witness'.

Keith normally partied till dawn, but one night in Clearwater, Florida, he was tired. A riff was going through his head, so he switched on his tape recorder. Then he fell asleep. 'The next morning I listened to the tape,' he recalls. 'There was about two minutes of an acoustic guitar playing a very rough riff of "Satisfaction" and then me snoring for 40 minutes.'

Keith admitted that the riff had been derived from a Motown record, namely Martha and the Vandellas' 'Dancing In The Street', which was later a chart-topper for Mick Jagger and David Bowie. The records, though, are markedly different. 'Dancing In The Street' was a song of happiness, while 'Satisfaction' was full of foreboding.

Keith played his riff to Jagger, who came up with the title. At first the song had a folk-rock feel, but then Mick realized it provided the opportunity for some anti-Establishment lyrics and he could speak for many of his fans. Effectively, he was writing a contemporary blues lyric and it was their first composition with a social content.

The Stones recorded four album tracks and a first take of 'Satisfaction' at a marathon 17-hour session at the Chess Studios. The next day they moved to Hollywood and completed the song during another gruelling session. Keith was unaware of the strength of what they'd recorded. He had used his new Gibson fuzzbox, but he was not happy. 'I wanted to cut it again but I don't think we could have done it right. You needed horns to really knock the riff out.' He also wasn't keen on the lyric. 'It was a working title. I never thought it was commercial enough to be a single.'

Nevertheless, it was released as a single in the US, but many stations were unhappy with the reference to 'I can't get no girl reaction'. When the Stones appeared on *The Ed Sullivan Show*, the phrase 'trying to make some girl' was bleeped. Even schoolteachers complained, as they disliked the double negative of 'I Can't Get No Satisfaction'. Mick had written it that way to underline his dissatisfaction. He railed against society, boring television, fraudulent advertising and his problems with girls. He had captured the mood of the times as succinctly as Pete Townshend with 'My Generation'.

The release of 'Satisfaction' was delayed in the UK, as Andrew Oldham wanted to ensure that the Beatles' 'Help!' had run its course. The pirate stations played it, and when it was released it quickly went to Number 1. Indeed, it made Number 1 in 38 different countries and sold over four million copies worldwide.

Keith was delighted when the song was covered by Otis Redding as he could now hear it with Memphis horns, but Mick only heard Otis demolish the lyric and destroy the song's meaning. Indeed, 'Satisfaction' sounds like a song that Otis Redding and Bob Dylan could have written together. Bob Dylan once told Keith, 'I could have written "Satisfaction" but you cats could never have written "Mr Tambourine Man".' Certainly, Dylan could have written the verses to 'Satisfaction', but could he have come up with such gut-wrenching rock'n'roll?

When a reporter asked Keith if he still had the tape on which he composed that magical riff, he said, 'No, tapes rot after 100 years, you know.'

First released:	1965
Highest UK chart position:	1
Highest US chart position:	1

'Keith made the riff up in Clearwater, Florida, not made it up, but I first heard it in Clearwater, Florida. He only had the first bit and then he had the riff, but it sounded like a country sort of thing on acoustic guitar, it didn't sound like rock. But he didn't really like it, he thought it was a joke, he didn't think it was a single or anything and that's the only **real** disagreement we've ever had.'

MICK JAGGER

good vibrations
beach boys

Having been pegged by the critics as a surf band who could only cut singles, the Beach Boys blew that premise apart with 'Pet Sounds', their own 'Sgt Pepper' one year upfront, which was more or less a Brian Wilson solo project with the group members chipping in their trademark harmonies when instructed. Yet rather than follow the album route, the rest of the year was spent polishing two singles to a startling intensity. Along with 'Heroes And Villains', 'Good Vibrations' almost transcended the 7-inch single form. This wasn't disposable pop, this was *art*!

Costing the then unprecedented sum of $16,000 to produce, in 17 different sessions at four LA studios, 'Vibrations' topped the charts on both sides of the Atlantic – and little wonder. From the wailing theremin (a rarely used keyboard instrument traditionally employed on horror-film soundtracks!) to the stunning vocal arrangement, it stakes a claim to be one of music's all-time great three minutes.

Unlike the majority of 'Pet Sounds', 'Good Vibrations' was clearly a team effort. The words, though, were somewhat longer in the making. Tony Asher had penned some verses during the 'Pet Sounds' sessions, but Mike Love, as lead singer, was eventually asked to come up with the final set of words.

And he left it late... 'I wrote the lyrics to "Good Vibrations" on the way down the Hollywood Freeway about ten minutes before the session. It was a unique experience, I was dictating the words as we were driving down the freeway. It's kind of amazing. It's one of those cliffhangers... We need some words, OK let's see!'

The song, Love admitted, was a 'radical departure for us musically' – and the words combined the fashionable hippie concept of 'vibes' with the more traditional boy-meets-girl theme. Brian Wilson, the Beach Boys' tortured musical genius, admitted the concept of vibrations 'scared me to death... my mother used to tell me about vibrations when I was a boy and I didn't really understand too much of what she meant... So we talked about good vibrations. On the one hand you could say these are sensual things... the extra-sensory perception that we have, that's what we're really talking about.'

The 20 musicians on the session didn't make head nor tail of it all either – Glen Campbell, then a session guitarist, encapsulated their feelings when he asked Wilson, 'Whew, Brian! What were you smokin' when you wrote that?' In fact, Wilson admits the influence of LSD was rather more of a contributory factor. For Beach Boy Bruce Johnston, 'We're either going to have the biggest hit in the world – or the Beach Boys' career is over.'

Capitol Records, Love recalls, 'weren't too crazy' about the result either... until it topped charts worldwide! In the UK, the *Sunday Express* headline summed it up – 'They've found a new sound at last!' Yet the song could well have ended up being recorded by future Three Dog Night singer Danny Hutton, who had heard it and expressed interest. It was this outside enthusiasm that had persuaded Brian Wilson to persevere with the song he saw as 'the summation of my musical vision, a harmonic convergence of imagination and talent, production values and craft, songwriting and spirituality.'

The success of 'Good Vibrations' rounded off a year in which the Beach Boys were voted World's Best Group in the annual *New Musical Express* readers' poll. Far more influential then than now, the paper's accolade meant a lot, especially as it was home-grown heroes the Beatles that they had beaten into second place! This was clearly something to savour, if not to spur Brian on to greater heights.

First released:	1966
Highest UK chart position:	1
Highest US chart position:	1

when a man loves a woman

percy sledge

Like so many soul stars of the 1960s, Percy Sledge will forever be associated with his biggest hit. His romantic ballad 'When A Man Loves A Woman' is an undisputed classic and remains his finest achievement. Born in Leighton, Alabama, in 1941, Sledge honed his emotive, gospel-tinged delivery at the Galilee Baptist Church on Sundays, working as a hospital orderly by day and fronting the Esquires Combo in the local clubs by night.

He had succeeded his cousin Jimmy Hughes in the role, and the measure of success he had enjoyed since going solo (notably the US Top 20 hit 'Steal Away') gave Percy the opportunity to dream of stardom.

'When A Man Loves A Woman' came about quite by accident when, after the break-up of an affair, he was too upset one night to sing the normal repertoire of cover versions. Improvising over a descending riff fashioned by bass player Calvin Lewis and organist Arthur Wright, he poured out his soul to devastating effect.

Later, he took the song (then called 'Why Did You Leave Me?') to local DJ-turned-producer Quin Ivy, who operated out of Sheffield, Alabama. The singer was so keen for a break that he auditioned in Ivy's Tune Town, the DJ's record shop. Impressed, Ivy took Percy into a studio he owned, teaming him with co-producer Marlin Greene on guitar and musicians from Rick Hall's Muscle Shoals school of legendary session men. In line with the change of title, the lyric received revision from Lewis before the tape rolled.

Recording engineer Jimmy Johnson claimed Percy 'was so out of tune we thought his voice might break a window!' Yet the combination of that plus a three-man horn section that was slightly off-pitch only seemed to accentuate the emotion of the song. The performance, captured around Christmas 1965, was a one-off. Atlantic supremo Jerry Wexler agreed, and the stage was set.

Issued on Atlantic in 1966, the single was a US Number 1 hit, establishing Percy Sledge nationally and providing the title for his debut album. He continued in the same vein for ensuing 45s, such as the country-tinged 'Warm And Tender Love' and 'Take Time To Know Her', but although he continued to record for Atlantic until 1973, diminishing returns swiftly set in.

But that wasn't the last we had heard of 'When A Man Loves A Woman' – and Percy was happy to step back into the spotlight when the song enjoyed a second lease of life courtesy of a Levi's UK TV commercial. It reached Number 2 in the UK, two places higher than originally, and was accompanied by 'When A Man Loves A Woman – The Ultimate Collection' (1987). Sadly for Sledge, he had neglected to take a share of the songwriting credit, so missed out on royalties when Michael Bolton took it back to the top in 1991 and won a Grammy into the bargain.

Sledge's original re-emerged the following year on the soundtrack of *The Crying Game*, while in 1993 BMI voted it their Song of the Year. Then, in 1994, came a Luis Mandoki motion picture that took the song not only as its theme but as its title. Sledge took this as his cue to return to recording on the PointBlank label with 'Blue Night' – an album which, along with a UK tour, proved that his gift for interpreting a song had only matured with the years. Unlike the sales figures of the song, the number of windows he had broken along the way remains uncertified.

First released:	1966
Highest UK chart position:	2
Highest US chart position:	1

love songs

all you need is love
beatles

I
f 1967 was the Summer of Love, then the Beatles' 'All You Need Is Love' has as much claim as anything to be the song of that summer. And it was quite literally an instant anthem, having been written specifically for an historic event – the very first worldwide simultaneous television broadcast by satellite. John and Paul decided to compose separate songs and then make a decision as to which one to use (although the Lennon-McCartney songwriting credit persisted, the pair were rarely collaborators at this point).

Paul's song (thought to have been 'Your Mother Should Know', but this has never been officially confirmed) was shelved in favour of the Lennon opus, which everyone agreed summed up the era most suitably: anything was possible, there's nothing you can do that can't be done… it's easy. This was an era when people thought music really *could* change the world.

The brief from the BBC had been succinct: keep it simple so that everyone everywhere will understand it. The international flavour of the broadcast was emphasized by an excerpt from the French national anthem, 'La Marseillaise', in the introduction. The instrumentation too was fairly exotic, John playing harpsichord (hired at a cost of ten guineas), Paul double bass and George violin.

Our World was scheduled to be beamed to viewers on five continents on Sunday 25 June 1967, and recording of the backing track at Olympic Studios began just 11 days earlier. The tenth of the 33 takes was deemed the best, and would be overdubbed with banjo and piano. Many people wrongly assume that the song appeared on the Beatles' groundbreaking 'Sgt Pepper's Lonely Hearts Club Band' album, but this was in fact issued on 1 July.

The scene shifted to Abbey Road on the 23rd, when the orchestra crammed into the large Number One studio and the Fab Four performed the vocals live to the result. Amazingly, the commercial potential only registered the day before the programme was aired, and the song would become the Beatles' fifteenth single.

On the day, the Beatles performed live over their pre-recorded backing track, assisted by an all-star choir sitting cross-legged in the Abbey Road studio that included Mick Jagger, Marianne Faithfull, Keith Richards, Keith Moon, Eric Clapton, Graham Nash and the Walker Brothers' Gary Leeds. A 13-piece orchestra was conducted by ex-Manfred Mann guitarist Mike Vickers, a classically trained musician with a foot in both cultural camps. Interestingly, horn player David Mason played the same piccolo trumpet that had featured so prominently in 'Penny Lane'. Only John Lennon's lead vocal would be re-recorded for the eventual release.

A potential 500 million audience had been diminished by 150 million when the Communist bloc dropped out… yet it was at Russia's suggestion that a copy of the full broadcast was deposited at the United Nations for posterity. The Beatles' section, lasting 6 minutes 11 seconds (3 minutes 40 seconds of which was the song itself) appeared under the heading of Artistic Excellence, one of several categories in the 125-minute broadcast (others included The Crowded World, This Hungry World and The World Beyond).

Paul McCartney summed up the whole venture thus: 'We'd been told we'd be seen recording it by the whole world at the same time so we had our message for the whole world – love – we need more love in the world.' A TV documentary series by Tony Palmer would later take the song as its title.

First released:	1967
Highest UK chart position:	1
Highest US chart position:	1

je t'aime... moi non plus

jane birkin & serge gainsbourg

The heavy-lidded, chain-smoking Serge Gainsbourg was one of the ugliest pop stars of all time, one of the most debauched – and, inevitably, one of the most interesting. His scandalous life was rarely out of the French press, and in 1997, six years after his death and with clever CD packaging, a cult has arisen and he has become a top-selling artist. His songs include '69 Année Erotique' and 'La Décadanse' with Jane Birkin, and 'Lemon Incest' with their 14-year-old daughter, Charlotte. He appeared on TV chat shows looking like a drunken intellectual down-and-out. On one occasion, he admitted that he wanted to sleep with the other guest, Whitney Houston.

In 1967, Gainsbourg wrote 'Je T'Aime... Moi Non Plus' as a duet for himself and Brigitte Bardot. The song involved much sensual groaning, and when Bardot took an acetate home, her husband Gunther Sachs said, 'You're making love to that man in the recording studio' and refused to sanction its release. Given half a chance, Gainsbourg would have recorded it that way.

Undeterred, Gainsbourg re-recorded it in London with his girlfriend, Jane Birkin, the former wife of film composer John Barry and the first actress to appear fully naked in a major film, *Blow Up*. As Gainsbourg murmurs on the record, 'L'amour physique est sans issue' or 'Nothing beats physical lovemaking'. Another line translates as 'I hold myself in check'. The record was banned by the BBC and condemned by the Vatican.

Despite, or perhaps because of the ban, 'Je T'Aime... Moi Non Plus' soared to Number 2, with an instrumental version by Sounds Nice also making the Top 20. The Fontana label, which was owned by Philips, then had second thoughts about the record and, in a burst of righteous indignation, deleted it. Major Minor, which was owned by Radio Caroline, had no such scruples: they reissued it and the record went to Number 1. It sold six million copies worldwide, but not many in the US through lack of airplay. The song prompted a witty parody from Frankie Howerd and June Whitfield, 'Up Je

T'Aime', where Whitfield was allegedly in bed with two men at the same time, and another in which Judge Dread falls for a transvestite. There is also 'Soul Je T'Aime' by Sylvia with Ralfi Pagan. All that heavy breathing came to good effect for Serge and Jane as their daughter, Charlotte, was born in 1971.

In 1976 Gainsbourg wrote and directed a film starring Jane Birkin called *Je T'Aime... Moi Non Plus*. It concerned a homosexual trucker who falls in love with a girl who looks like a boy. The film was controversial for Birkin's ear-splitting shrieks when she is subjected to anal sex. The reverse of the song, in fact. Jane Birkin and Brigitte Bardot had a lesbian bed scene in the film *Ms Don Juan* and, to show her versatility, Birkin also made a series of popular French comedy films.

In 1995 Birkin appeared in the National Theatre's production of *The Women Of Troy*. Charlotte is now an established film actress and featured in *The Cement Garden*, directed by Jane's brother, Andrew, and *Jane Eyre*, directed by Franco Zeffirelli. A biography, *Gainsbourg Sans Filter*, dwelt on Serge's carousing, and Mick Harvey recorded an album of his songs in English called 'Intoxicated Man'. Jane Birkin has a cabaret show of his songs. 'He wrote in one of them, "One day you'll know that I gave you the best of me". And he did. He liked to sing provocative songs himself and he gave me the sad ones.'

First released:	1969
Highest UK chart position:	1
Highest US chart position:	–

In some ways, the success of 'Bridge Over Troubled Water' has proved a millstone for writer Paul Simon, who elected singing partner Art Garfunkel to perform it as the title track of the duo's last album together. Its release at the end of the peace-and-love 1960s came just weeks before the Beatles' similarly spiritual swansong 'Let It Be', and the song inspired other rock and religion links like 'Morning Has Broken', 'My Sweet Lord' and 'Desiderata'.

Although a pop song, 'Bridge Over Troubled Water' has its roots firmly in the gospel tradition: Simon himself claimed to have borrowed the title from a song by the Swan Silvertones called 'Mary Don't You Weep', in which lead singer Claude Jeter's vocal improvisation caught the composer's ear. 'Had it not been for him I would never have written "Bridge Over Troubled Water"… The guy has probably the best falsetto voice in the world.'

Written on guitar, 'Bridge' initially had the working title of 'Hymn', but when string arranger Jimmy Haskell transposed it for piano he misheard its new title and headed his sheet music 'Like A Pitcher Of Water' (an amused Simon later had this framed).

bridge over troubled water

simon and garfunkel

The song was written in the summer of 1969, when Simon and his then wife Peggy rented a house on Blue Jay Way in Los Angeles – the same house where George Harrison had earlier written 'Blue Jay Way'. Lyrically, there were originally only two verses, but a third was added in the studio for balance: Simon has always considered this to be below the standard of the others. The line 'Sail on silver girl' was interpreted by some as referring to drugs, specifically a hypodermic syringe, but the writer was in fact offering reassurance to his wife who had recently discovered her first grey hairs!

The song's instrumental track – dominated by the piano of one-time Elvis Presley sideman Larry Knechtel – was laid down in Los Angeles, with the vocals added after the duo returned to New York. The distinctive, slowly building arrangement was inspired by Phil Spector's treatment of 'Ol' Man River' for the Righteous Brothers, utilizing a gospel chorus but holding it back until late in the song for maximum impact.

Unusually, 'Bridge' was premiered before its recording on the *Bell Telephone Hour*, a Simon and Garfunkel TV special that turned from a greatest hits showcase into a biting state-of-the-nation commentary. Broadcast in November 1969, it was never repeated due to the controversy it stirred.

The song titled the first single and album ever to top the UK and US single and album charts simultaneously. It was Simon and Garfunkel's third and final US Number 1 single after 'The Sound Of Silence' (1966) and 'Mrs Robinson' (1967), and by the end of its first year of release the single alone had earned Simon an estimated $7 million.

The duo split after touring in support of the album, ensuring that Simon didn't have to top his classic. 'I'm delighted I didn't have to write a Simon and Garfunkel follow-up to "Bridge Over Troubled Water" which I think would have been an inevitable letdown,' he later admitted. But when Simon and Garfunkel did finally reform in 1981 for a concert in New York's Central Park, the song was an inevitable highlight. They reprised it yet again in February 1990 when they were inducted into the Rock'n'Roll Hall of Fame in New York.

No matter what may lie in the future for one of the major songwriters of the rock era, Paul Simon will never top 'Bridge Over Troubled Water' for its success, ubiquity and earning power. It has been recorded by over 200 artists, its words have been quoted in presidential campaigns and undoubtedly served as inspiration and comfort to many of the millions who bought it – yet the irony remains that, despite the peace and tranquillity it evokes, 'Bridge' was recorded at a time when the partnership of Simon and Garfunkel was about to split permanently and irrevocably.

First released:	1970
Highest UK chart position:	1
Highest US chart position:	1

love songs

James Taylor is the King of Bedsit Rock. In the 1970s – and maybe to this day – young people, alone in bedrooms and getting over love affairs, would put on laid-back albums by the sensitive singer-songwriter. In fact, the honey-voiced Taylor was so laid back that he was almost horizontal. His self-pitying, introspective songs might make listeners feel worse, but that was the point. Leonard Cohen was too bleak and suicidal for some, but everyone agreed that James Taylor, who never sounded wide awake, was just right. The key album was 1970's 'Sweet Baby James'. Taylor was so big that record company executives signed up the rest of his family.

The thin and gaunt Taylor was only 22 when he made 'Sweet Baby James' but he had crammed a lifetime of suffering into five years. There had been broken relationships, heroin addiction and time in a mental institution. Not to mention Apple Records. He had come to England in 1968 and was given a record contract by

fire and rain

james taylor

Paul McCartney. He disliked the lavish production on his Apple album and wanted something more acoustic-based, but he stayed friendly with the producer, Peter Asher (previously half of saccharine duo Peter and Gordon), who then arranged a deal with Warner Brothers.

'Sweet Baby James' was full of restrained playing and minor-key melodies. It included the pessimistic, somewhat desperate 'Fire And Rain'. The first verse, a tender eulogy for his friend Suzanne, was written while he was living in London's Notting Hill. He went back on heroin – well, Notting Hill was hardly the best venue for an ex-addict in 1968 – and returned to America for treatment. The second verse was written in a hospital room in Manhattan with his body aching and his time at hand. He asks Jesus to help him, but this is bitterly ironic as he mocked those who sought religion. Taylor completed the song in the Austin Riggs Hospital in Stockbridge, Massachusetts. He is planning for his future and the reference to flying machines is to his first group, the Flying Machine.

The song became a US Top 10 hit, and although it only scrambled into the UK Top 50, it is regarded as a standard. Taylor has to perform it at every concert, and on his 1985 album 'That's Why I'm Here' he sings: 'Fortune and fame is such a curious game/Perfect strangers can call you by name/Pay good money to hear "Fire And Rain"/Again and again and again.'

Strangely, James Taylor tended to have more success with cover versions – 'You've Got A Friend', 'How Sweet It Is', 'Handy Man', 'Up On The Roof' and 'Mockingbird' with his wife, Carly Simon. He wrote pithy, reflective lyrics and, considering the times they worked together, it is unfortunate that he and Carole King didn't write songs together. He even wrote a song about writing songs, 'Hey Mister That's Me Up On The Jukebox'. He said, 'At the time, I didn't think my songs were personal. Generally speaking, the songs to me seemed like love songs. Years later, I don't deny it. The stuff I write does come from an autobiographical place.'

As the years went by and Taylor became comfortable in his new role as a parent with Carly Simon, the nature of his songwriting changed. 'I didn't want my son being asked, "What does your daddy do?" and replying, "He plays the guitar and he talks about his drug problems."' When Carly Simon topped the charts with 'You're So Vain', there was much speculation over the song's subject, although it was most likely a composite picture. Was it Warren Beatty or Mick Jagger? At the time, no one suggested James Taylor, but with his self-centred songs he must be a candidate.

First released:	1970
Highest UK chart position:	42
Highest US chart position:	3

love songs

without you
nilsson

ew songs become transatlantic chart-toppers; fewer still twice over. Any writer of such a song would, by all rights, be 'set up for life' on the royalties. But the success of 'Without You', a Number 1 for both Nilsson in 1972 and Mariah Carey in 1994, did little for Pete Ham and Tommy Evans' peace of mind. Both ended their own lives, depressed at the problems that had brought their group, Badfinger, to its knees. And far from being the men with the Midas touch, as had seemed the case when the Beatles signed them to their Apple label, they became two of rock'n'roll's most tragic casualties.

The song started life as just another album track on the group's 1970 offering, 'No Dice'. American singer Harry Nilsson had heard it and liked it, but mistakenly thought it was a Beatles tune – understandable since, as well as being Apple artists, Badfinger's musicians had sessioned for George Harrison and John Lennon, while Paul McCartney had written and produced their first hit 'Come And Get It' (from the film *The Magic Christian*).

'Without You' gained in stature with Nilsson's stately interpretation, when compared with the frankly shambolic Badfinger version, suggesting that the American's producer/arranger Richard Perry deserves a share of the reflected glory. It was a true collaboration by the writers, guitarist Ham suggesting that a chorus which bassist Evans had written could be amalgamated with his verses. These had emerged after he had let down his girlfriend and gone to the studio to record, instead of taking her on a long-postponed night out. 'He said he was really sorry, that he'd make it up to me,' Beverly Ellis later revealed. 'I told him it was all right… and he said "Your mouth's smiling, but your eyes are not." When they finished the song the next day he was very pleased with it… that line, "You always smile but in your eyes your sorrow shows", was about what happened.'

The song's tragic mood has been enhanced by subsequent events. There was disharmony both within the band and outside, the former arising because although there had been an informal agreement that writing royalties would be shared for the group's hits, this had been a hit by another artist. There was also a minefield of legal red tape surrounding the band, including a separate management contract for the US where the band were most popular as a 'surrogate Beatles', and very little money was percolating through the system from either side of the Atlantic to keep Ham and Evans solvent.

The pair, who lived near each other in Surrey, had a drinking session one night in April 1975 and apparently decided to quit. A phone call to the States having proved inconclusive, the next morning Ham was found hanged in his garage, his last reported words to Evans being 'I know a way out. I'll see you again.'

Sickened by the tragedy, Evans quit music for three years but re-formed the band in 1978, signing with a new American manager. But money was again in short supply and the band returned to the UK, where they were served with a lawsuit for breaking their contract. Amid all this, a growth in his throat had given Evans further cause for concern and, after an evening spent singing Everly Brothers songs with his wife Marianne, he too ended his life. It is said that the police thought the lyric sheet they found (written out by Evans for his wife's benefit) was a suicide note.

The legal fallout is still settling, but the financial rewards are still accruing – to someone. Over 100 cover versions of the song have put it in the 'Yesterday' league (ironic, given the Apple connection), while thanks to Mariah Carey's syrupy soul cover it was certified as Most Played Song of 1994 by the American Society of Composers, Authors and Publishers. But, bizarrely, by that point the other two Badfinger members, guitarist Joey Molland and drummer Mike Gibbins, along with UK manager Bill Collins, had been declared joint copyright holders in the song, and received plaques commemorating the award.

Bob Jackson, who joined the group on keyboards in 1974, says, 'The story of Badfinger encapsulates every awful story you've ever heard about rock'n'roll.' Plus at least one great song…

First released:	1972
Highest UK chart position:	1
Highest US chart position:	1

love will tear us apart

joy division

The seeds that grew up to become Joy Division were first planted in late 1976 when Ian Curtis, Bernard Albrecht, Peter Hook and Steve Brotherdale formed themselves into the Stiff Kittens. The group never performed live, and by May 1977 had changed their name to Warsaw (in honour of a David Bowie album track) and made their live debut at Manchester's Electric Circus. The discovery that there was another group, based in London, with the name Warsaw Pakt prompted yet another monicker change, this time to Joy Division. This was taken from a novel, *House Of Dolls*, and was the name given to Nazi concentration-camp prostitutes. The origins of the name ensured the group maximum publicity thereafter.

Over the next 18 months or so the group established a reputation as a live act and attracted considerable record company interest, although little was actually released on vinyl. A self-funded EP on their own Enigma label, one track on a Virgin compilation and another two tracks on a Factory compilation were pretty much the full extent of the group on record, so when 'Unknown Pleasures' finally appeared in July 1979 on the Factory label it was eagerly awaited. It promptly took up residence in the independent chart and led to an increasing number of live dates for the group.

This, in turn, is perhaps where the root of later problems for the group began, for the demands placed upon lead vocalist and chief songwriter Ian Curtis, who suffered from epilepsy, became greater. By 1980, matters had pretty much reached a peak, for a number of European dates had to be cancelled because of Curtis' deteriorating health and he was helped off the stage at what proved to be the group's final live concert in May. One month earlier, they had released 'Love Will Tear Us Apart', a haunting and yet powerful single which was hailed a smash by the media.

Although the single did top the independent charts, it failed to cross over into the pop charts, an event that appeared to devastate Curtis. Four days before the group were due to fly to the US for their first-ever American live dates, he hanged himself at his home. Ironically, this action brought about the commercial acceptance of Joy Division's work that Curtis had been so desperate to achieve: 'Love Will Tear Us Apart' was re-released and made Number 13 in July 1980.

Curtis' death and the belated success of the single effectively made Joy Division's reputation; when the group subsequently changed name again to New Order (a name with similar Nazi connotations, although the group denied it), they were established as one of the pioneering acts of the age. 'Love Will Tear Us Apart' proved enduring enough to re-chart on two further occasions (a Number 19 placing in November 1981 and Number 19 again when remixed in 1995), while there have been three cover versions: by Paul Young, Swan and P.J. Proby (Proby's version included contributions from former Joy Division member Peter Hook).

First released:	1980
Highest UK chart position:	13
Highest US chart position:	—

love songs

In 1975 John Lennon had a musical lay-off to become a house-husband, baking bread and bringing up his son, Sean. Some say he had hit a creative block, but maybe he had had enough of the lunacy of his producer, Phil Spector, who had put him off recording studios. Whatever the reason, 'Double Fantasy', 'A heart play by John Lennon and Yoko Ono' and his first album for five years, showed he was still capable of writing good songs.

The songs started to flow in June 1980 when John, Yoko and Sean were on holiday in Bermuda. He captured his love for Yoko in 'Woman' and sang a lullaby to Sean, 'Beautiful Boy (Darling Boy)'. Its message was that life is what happens while you're making other plans. So, unfortunately, is death.

John and Yoko started recording in August – every John Lennon song was matched by one from Yoko. John's ambition was to get her a Number 1 single, and according to biographer Albert Goldman, 'The ultimate irony was that Yoko came off sounding better than John.' The album was named 'Double Fantasy' after a flower they had seen in a botanical garden.

(just like)
starting over

john
lennon

John started writing frantically, but rejected many of his songs. He took elements of three of them – 'My Life', 'Don't Be Crazy' and 'The Worst Is Over' – and came up with '(Just Like) Starting Over'. It advocated a second honeymoon of passionate lovemaking and one discarded line was 'The time has come, the Walrus said, for you and I to stay in bed'.

John was still a rocker: 'It was a 1950s sound because I'd never really recorded a song that sounded like that period, although that was my period, the music I identified with. In my Beatle days, that would have been taken as a joke. One avoided clichés, but now these clichés are not clichés anymore.' Shades of Sun rockabilly, Roy Orbison and the Beach Boys can be heard in the arrangement, and again Goldman was not amused: 'a contrived and campy throwback to a style of long ago, the song was merely a bit of fluff.'

JOHN LENNON SHOT DEAD

Gunned down by 'screwball' outside home as wife Yoko watches in horror

DRAMATIC COVERAGE: PAGES 2, 3, 4, 5, 31, 32, 33

'Some people took "Starting Over" serious, saying, "What's he trying to do and all that?" but they forget I've had tongue-in-cheek all along, I am the walrus, all of them had tongue-in-cheek. Just because other people see depths of whatever's in it, what does it really mean? I am the egg man, could have been the pudding basin for all I care, it's just tongue-in-cheek.'

JOHN LENNON

The studio conversation leading up to the final take has emerged on a bootleg. John is in tremendous form, parodying his own lyrics ('It's been so long since we've been apart/My feet are hurting, I start to fart') and teasing the bass player for not sounding 1950s enough. Just before the take, he says, 'This one's for Gene and Eddie and Elvis'.

The title was perfect for John's comeback and he put a bell at its start, sounding like a kitchen timer. 'The head of the album is a wishing bell of Yoko's. It's like the beginning of "Mother" on the first album, which had a very slow death bell. It's taken a long time to get from one bell to the other, but that's the connection. My work is one piece.'

The US single of '(Just Like) Starting Over' was at Number 6 and going up on 8 December 1980. In the UK, it had gone to Number 8 but fallen back to Number 21. That night John and Yoko were walking back from the Hit Factory, where they had been mixing 'Walking On

Thin Ice' for a second album. As they entered the Dakota Building, someone called out, 'Mr Lennon?' and shot him five times. Ironically, '(Just Like) Starting Over' had been John's downfall. Mark Chapman lived as an ersatz John Lennon and having the real John back in public disturbed his mind.

The title now is grimly ironic – but that often happens. At the time of their deaths, Hank Williams was pushing 'I'll Never Get Out Of This World Alive', Buddy Holly 'It Doesn't Matter Anymore', Elvis Presley 'Way Down' and Eddie Cochran 'Three Steps To Heaven'.

First released:	1980
Highest UK chart position:	1
Highest US chart position:	1

The success of the Police in jumping on to the late-1970s punk bandwagon had been proof that you *could* teach old dogs new tricks. Drummer Stewart Copeland and guitarist Andy Summers were music-business veterans with pasts they took care to conceal: yet by 1983, when the Sex Pistols *et al* were firmly part of rock history, their musicianship allied to the songs of bassist-vocalist Gordon Sumner, better known as Sting, had established them firmly among the élite.

The band's successful musical formula of the early days had consisted of grafting meaty, beaty punk choruses on to laid-back, reggae-styled verses. Yet 'Every Breath You Take' – released as a single in May 1983 shortly before the fifth Police album, 'Synchronicity', hit the world's record racks – was relatively straightforward in musical form with its relentless mid-tempo beat.

every breath you take

police

Reviewing the effort, *The Times* described it as 'A couple of bars' worth of music, a strong central thought and two minutes with a rhyming dictionary producing a perfect pop construction.' Yet that simplicity belied the fact that an elaborate synthesizer arrangement had been devised, only to be axed at the last moment so as not to detract from the simple, straightforward effect. After years of trying, Sting had created that perfect paradox – a pop song that worked on more than one level.

Many of those who bought the song considered it a hymn of devotion, the singer following in his loved one's footsteps like a faithful hound. But a scan of the lyrics (included in a Police album package for the first time) suggested otherwise. Its writer described the song as 'A song of experience, about jealousy and possession… a sinister, evil song veiled in a romantic setting.'

Once this inner truth was revealed, the press seized on the malevolence of the lyric as an indication of Sting's state of mind after a recent divorce from actress wife Frances Tomelty. But that was, perhaps, naive: after all, he had been a happily married man when he penned the words for songs like 'Can't Stand Losing You', 'So Lonely' and 'Hole In My Life' that had endeared the Police to millions worldwide.

The iciness of the delivery made it surprising that the sun of Montserrat had been the recording venue and not Abba's Polar Studios, the other choice. The song had been written in similarly idyllic surroundings – the

Jamaican hideaway of Golden Eye – at the self-same desk where 007's creator Ian Fleming had plotted and planned James Bond's next move.

With the Police's members having dispersed to follow individual projects for the previous 18 months – an eternity in pop terms – it was, Copeland admitted, 'good to be back in business… everyone thought we had broken up or something.' Sting was more forceful: 'All the bastards wrote us off, and I knew I had this song. I knew it would be a Number 1.' A transatlantic chart-topper no less – their first US Number 1 and fifth at home. The American success was particularly long lived, eight weeks making it joint second to 'Hey Jude' as the most enduring chart-topper from a British band. It returned to the top in 1997 in the hands of rap artist Puff Daddy and Faith Evans, albeit with new lyrics, entitled 'I'll Be Missing You'.

Sting would refer back to the song twice: firstly in a joky coda ('every cake you bake, every leg you break') to his 1985 solo hit 'Love Is The Seventh Wave', and again later in the decade, when he altered the lyrics for the satirical TV puppet show *Spitting Image* to 'Every Bomb You Make' in protest against the arms race. In 1986, the song had titled a Greatest Hits package that effectively signalled the band were no more. Having created the perfect pop song, Sting had called it a day and moved on.

First released:	1983
Highest UK chart position:	1
Highest US chart position:	1

love songs

After the excesses of the punk era of the 1970s, the 1980s saw pop music back in vogue, in particular a slew of attractively packaged acts with attractively packaged albums. Leading the way in the UK were the likes of Duran Duran, Spandau Ballet and Wham!. And while America had not succumbed to punk, there was definitely room for Duran Duran, Wham! and their ilk.

Wham! had first emerged in 1982 with a number of rap songs that had captured the imagination of the young record-buying public, although the group, ostensibly George Michael and Andrew Ridgeley with a changing duo of female backing singers, had been writing material together since 1979. Although their single releases invariably carried the joint credit of Michael/Ridgeley, there was little doubt that George Michael was chiefly responsible.

'Careless Whisper' was one of those songs George had written in 1979, although he did not feel confident enough to record it until some considerable time later. The song had already been chosen as the ideal vehicle

careless whisper

george michael

with which to launch his solo career, so in 1983 he flew to America in order to work with producer Jerry Wexler at the Muscle Shoals Studios in Alabama. Although the sessions were extremely instructive for the singer, they were also unsuccessful, and he decided to produce the song himself. The revised version sounded much better, as George discovered when he tested out the record.

'The very last night I worked as a DJ I played the demo of "Careless Whisper". I knew it didn't matter if I got into trouble because I had already given in my notice the week before. So right at the end of the night, I played it and the floor filled. They had never heard it before and the floor filled. I remember thinking, "That's a good sign." And I wondered what was going to happen to that song.'

What happened is relatively simple: it topped the UK charts for three weeks, selling over a million copies in the process. (In addition to becoming George/Wham!'s first million-seller, it was also his record label's first UK million-seller – and this was the label that could boast the likes of Abba and Michael Jackson.) George was happy. 'We knocked off Duran Duran from Number 1, then Frankie Goes To Hollywood knocked us off, then "Careless Whisper" knocked them off. I really loved that. I never felt threatened. I must admit I never thought the

Frankies would be around for very long. All the English bands were dependent on other people for songwriting, production, you name it.'

The single was also a huge US success, selling another million copies and also topping the charts for three weeks. In 1985, an emotional George collected two awards that reflected the success of 'Careless Whisper' in particular: the Ivor Novello Award for Songwriter of the Year and Most Performed Work. George later said, '"Careless Whisper" was not an integral part of my emotional development. It's sad because that song means so much to so many people. It disappoints me that you can write a lyric very flippantly – and not a particularly good lyric – and it can mean so much to so many people. That's disillusioning for a writer.'

Not surprisingly, the song has become the staple diet of karaoke and nightclubs ever since.

First released:	1984
Highest UK chart position:	1
Highest US chart position:	1

'If you listen to "Careless Whisper" and then listen to any one of the Wham! singles and then tell me that Wham! and George Michael are the same thing, then you have faulty hearing. I think it was the right time to release it because our profile is very high now and it's an old song that we wanted to get out of the way, because we've got better stuff to release. But it would have been very, very stupid as a Wham! record.'

GEORGE MICHAEL

love songs

O n 13 July 1991, the cumbersomely titled but ultra-romantic '(Everything I Do) I Do It For You' displaced Jason Donovan's jaunty 'Any Dream Will Do' to top the UK chart – and would stay there for a record 16 weeks. The ballad, originally intended for a female singer like Kate Bush or Lisa Stansfield to record, had been penned by singer Bryan Adams, producer Robert 'Mutt' Lange and filmscore specialist Michael Kamen as the central theme to Kevin Costner's blockbuster movie, *Robin Hood: Prince Of Thieves*, after Kamen had sent Adams a tune he had originally written back in the 1960s. Adams and Lange added lyrics and, instead of using medieval instruments, gave the song rock instrumentation that included Little Feat's Billy Payne on keyboards.

The resulting hit was the first single to sell a million in the UK since Jennifer Rush's 'The Power Of Love' in 1985, and Adams was the fifth Canadian – behind Paul Anka (1957), Terry Jacks (1974), J.J. Barrie (1976) and

(everything i do)
i do it for you

bryan
adams

Alannah Myles (1990) – to achieve the feat. Later in July it hit the US Number 1 spot and remained there for seven weeks, becoming the country's second biggest-selling single ever. It subsequently topped the pile in 16 countries, selling over eight million copies worldwide and becoming one of the most successful singles of all time. With a new Adams album still some months away, the *Robin Hood* soundtrack became an unexpected bestseller in its stead.

'I can't believe my single has been at Number 1 for longer than the Beatles and the Stones,' a bemused Bryan told *The Sun* newspaper. 'This is the biggest thing that ever happened to me. Now I'm waiting for my prize, something like those championship belts boxers wear. I hope Slim Whitman hasn't lost it after all this time!' Tracked down by the tabloids, the 1950s country star whose record Adams eclipsed was surprisingly happy at being written out of the record books. 'He's done a great job,' he stated approvingly, adding: 'I'm pleased for him.'

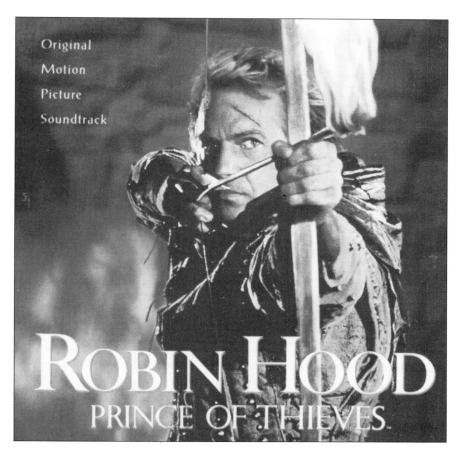

Original
Motion
Picture
Soundtrack

ROBIN HOOD
PRINCE OF THIEVES

An equally happy sequel came in November 1991 when Bryan invited Slim to fly, all expenses paid, from his home in Florida to sing the previous record-holder, 'Rose Marie' from 1955, to an open-mouthed audience at a Wembley Arena concert. Whitman, who admitted it was his first-ever experience of a rock'n'roll show, travelled home whistling a new tune…

But then came the big ones – not only the Grammies but the Oscars – for which 'I Do It For You' was eligible by virtue of its film-theme status. Part one of the masterplan fell into place when, on 25 February, the recording was duly acclaimed as the Best Song Written Specifically for a Motion Picture or for Television. Sadly, an Academy Award would not be forthcoming, despite Adams performing live at the ceremony: Disney's saccharine 'Beauty And The Beast' took the honours there.

The *Billboard* Music Awards, held in Santa Monica the previous December, had seen 'I Do It For You' win the Top World Single, Top Adult Contemporary Single and Top Hot 100 Single categories, while April would see Adams receive the ultimate songwriting accolade, an Ivor Novello Award, at the Grosvenor House Hotel in London. From then on, he, Lange and Kamen were much in demand in Hollywood, and contributed further themes to *The Three Musketeers* (the US chart-topping 'All For One'), *Don Juan de Marco* ('Have You Ever Really Loved A Woman') and Disney's *Jack* ('Star').

First released:	1991
Highest UK chart position:	1
Highest US chart position:	1

41

Country music is not known for feminist anthems – quite the reverse, when you consider the servile 'Born A Woman' and 'Stand By Your Man'. True, there's Loretta Lynn's 'The Pill', but she's only cheating because her man cheated first. With an audience of blue-collar workers, such male domination is hardly surprising. What is unexpected is the new life put into 1990s country music by several self-respecting women. k.d. lang was shunned by Nashville for admitting she was a lesbian, but that would not happen to a performer now. Rosanne Cash encouraged the bruised protagonist of 'Rosie Strikes Back' to leave her vicious husband. Michelle Wright laid down the ground rules for her partner in 'Take It Like A Man'.

he thinks he'll keep her

mary-chapin carpenter

A million-dollar bash of country stars conventionally ends with them singing 'Will The Circle Be Unbroken?', but the 1993 Women of Country concert concluded with a fierce rendition of Mary-Chapin Carpenter's 'The Hard Way'. The opening act was Carpenter herself: her song, 'He Thinks He'll Keep Her'. Both came from her fourth album, 'Come On, Come On', released in 1992. As so often, the songs were fuelled by her own experiences and her desire for self-discovery.

Some argue that Carpenter is not a country artist at all: she specializes in slow ballads and her music embraces many genres. She told the *Daily Telegraph*, 'I occupy an indefinable area, and no one's invented a term for it yet, as someone who grew up with country, folk, rock, blues, pop and bluegrass. With me, it's all in there somewhere.' She also says, 'Labels are for soup cans.'

'He Thinks He'll Keep Her' was written with an established Nashville writer, Don Schlitz ('The Gambler', 'Forever And Ever, Amen' and 'When You Say Nothing At All'). They wrote four songs for the album, including 'He Thinks He'll Keep Her'. The song describes a long-standing marriage in which the husband has denied his wife the right to any feelings or expression. She spends her time washing clothes, making meals and transporting children: 'Everything runs right on time, years of practice and design.' The husband doesn't suspect that anything is wrong, then 'When she was 36, she met him at the door, She said, "I'm sorry, I don't love you anymore."' It's beautifully observed, with a resolutely upbeat, defiant chorus, and naturally has been hijacked by feminists. Carpenter says, 'I feel sorry for both the characters in the song. She allowed the situation to develop; it's both their faults.'

At first Columbia Records was reluctant to issue it as a country single, as it was feared that radio stations would regard it as a man-hating song. It wasn't released until 1994 and then spent four months gradually climbing the US country charts, eventually reaching Number 4. This in itself must be considered an achievement: the truck drivers had taken to it after all.

There are many diverse female talents to be heard in Nashville today – Suzy Bogguss, Deana Carter, Patty Loveless, Kathy Mattea, Pam Tillis, Trisha Yearwood and more established artists like Reba McEntire, Nanci Griffith, Emmylou Harris and Wynonna Judd. The glitzy

rhinestone image of Dolly Parton is outdated, although she addresses contemporary issues in her songs, a recent one being about PMT. Mary-Chapin Carpenter says of today's country, 'It's not as simplistic as my guy left me and I'm sitting in the bar playing the jukebox. The issues are edgier and more compelling. The music is very brave and interesting and to me that's real life.'

First released:	1992
Highest UK chart position:	71
Highest US chart position:	–

Most people like something to suck on while they're watching a film at the cinema, and Alanis Morissette is no exception. The Canadian songstress hit the headlines in 1995 with her third album, 'Jagged Little Pill' – specifically the track 'You Oughta Know', which tells how she performed oral sex on her boyfriend in a movie theatre, only to be swiftly dumped for a newer model soon afterwards. After witnessing the ex-boyfriend proudly parading his new flame, Alanis challenged them both in a restaurant and demanded: 'It was a slap in the face how quickly I was replaced/And are you thinking of me when you fuck her?'

As if that wasn't enough to turn their Peking duck into sweet'n'sour, she follows up with the controversial lines: 'Is she perverted like me/Would she go down on you in a theatre?' If it were not God's honest truth, you could justly accuse Alanis Morissette of downright sensationalism, but she swears that it really happened.

you oughta know

alanis morissette

'I did do that, it's true, I went right down on him in a movie theatre,' Morissette shrugs. 'Yeah, I was a little worried about putting that incident into a song, but I don't believe in censoring anything, so I used it. It was something I had to do, this whole album came from a place inside of me. But it all boils down to the fact that I want to walk through life, not get dragged through it.'

Besides being a great song in its own right, 'You Oughta Know' is also a remarkably honest piece of lyricism, providing a useful warning for the average male over the way a 1990s female will react when she's treated disrespectfully. Despite claims that 'You Oughta Know' is 'not about revenge', she insists on demanding of her ex-lover: 'Every time I scratch my nails down someone else's back/I hope you feel it'. And doubtless he does.

Such lyrical intensity would be wasted if unaccompanied by a musical spirit. Fortunately for Alanis and her co-lyricist/producer Glenn Ballard (who has subsequently enhanced his reputation by working with Aerosmith and Van Halen), they persuaded none other than Flea and Dave Navarro of the Red Hot Chili Peppers to guest on the track, bringing to it a warming, fluent groove.

But beside all this anger and bitterness, 'Jagged Little Pill' contains numerous astute observations on real-life situations, from puzzlement at her Catholic church upbringing to the false promises of the music industry. However, it also manages to celebrate the joy and contentment of finding the right person. Comparing the confrontational lyrics and take-no-shit attitudes with the innocuous nature of her first two LPs (1990's 'Alanis' and 1992's 'Now Is The Time' – only available in Canada, and described by the lady herself as 'more pop than rock'), the critics have judged Morissette harshly as some kind of post-grunge opportunist. She refutes such accusations, while admitting that she hasn't always found it easy to address these difficult subjects.

'In the past I have denied myself any revelling in my darker side,' she says. 'But as soon as I started writing, I came to terms with it. If you're too precious, you lose the spirit in which the song was written.'

First released:	1995
Highest UK chart position:	22
Highest US chart position:	–

love is all around

wet wet wet

I f ever a record was an apt theme tune for a group, then it was surely 'Wild Thing' by the Troggs. Although they didn't write the song (that privilege rested with American songwriter Chip Taylor), it was for many years the one with which they were always associated. And why not – it had been a UK Number 2 and a US chart-topper. The group had similarly lived up to the image conveyed by the single: in an age when there were also the Rolling Stones, the Troggs were the original wild men of rock.

Lead vocalist and chief songwriter Reg Presley exemplified that image more than most, and so it was hard to imagine him sitting at home on a Sunday afternoon, quietly watching television and getting inspiration for his songwriting from the regular fare that was offered on the channels. For some reason, Reg (originally born with the name Reg Ball – journalist Keith Altham suggested changing it to Presley, rightly reasoning that the media would latch on to it once the group became famous) was watching a religious programme one afternoon and constructed a song based on a Salvation Army chant, 'love is all around'. The final single was a radical departure from 'Wild Thing', but the Troggs were popular enough for it to become a UK Number 5 and US Number 7 in 1968. There the story of the song might have ended, but it was all resurrected in 1994.

By the 1990s, a successful film was judged not only by how much it grossed at the cinema but also by how many hit singles it could spawn. *The Bodyguard* and *Robin Hood: Prince Of Thieves*, for example, had given us 'I Will Always Love You' and '(Everything I Do) I Do It For You' by Whitney Houston and Bryan Adams respectively, and both singles were among the longest-running Number 1s in the UK. Scottish group Wet Wet Wet, who had already scored two UK chart-toppers, were invited to revive 'Love Is All Around' for the 1994 film *Four Weddings And A Funeral*, a low-budget comedy starring Hugh Grant and Andie MacDowell. Despite the quintessentially British storyline, the film went on to become the highest-grossing UK-made movie of all time, and the success of the single undoubtedly fuelled interest in the film (and vice versa).

As it was, Wet Wet Wet's treatment of 'Love Is All Around' stormed the charts, hitting the top in June and looking to all intents and purposes as though it had taken up residence. It had already logged up 15 weeks at the summit and looked likely to topple Bryan Adams' longevity record of 16, when Wet Wet Wet announced that the single was to be deleted with immediate effect. This was a somewhat surprising move, for it was reasoned that the object of a single was to sell, which 'Love Is All Around' had done spectacularly (over one million copies in the UK alone, where it was awarded a double platinum disc). It was later revealed by lead vocalist Marti Pellow that the group had grown tired of the song, having been exposed to it so many times, and they figured the rest of the general public must feel the same way.

Despite the decision to delete the record, songwriter Reg Presley was a very happy man. Aside from the royalties the song had attracted, he finally got the recognition he felt he deserved; at the Ivor Novello Awards in 1995 'Love Is All Around' was named the PRS (Performing Rights Society) Most Performed Work, Bestselling Song and International Hit of the Year. The original wild man had much for which to thank the Salvation Army!

First released:	1994
Highest UK chart position:	1
Highest US chart position:	41

sweet little sixteen

chuck berry

Although rock'n'roll owes its origin to black rhythm and blues, few black performers became stars themselves. Little Richard, Fats Domino and, most of all, Chuck Berry were exceptions. Between 1955 and 1958, Chuck had US Top 10 hits with 'Maybellene', 'Schoolday', 'Rock And Roll Music', 'Sweet Little Sixteen', 'Johnny B Goode' and 'Carol', all of which became rock'n'roll standards. Whenever musicians jam together, they pick Chuck Berry songs, and what guitarist doesn't want to play that 15-second introduction to 'Johnny B Goode'?

Surprisingly, few people in Britain bought Chuck Berry's records at the time. His only UK Top 20 success during the 1950s was with 'Sweet Little Sixteen', which was in the charts for five weeks and peaked at sweet little 16. Keith Fordyce, writing in the *New Musical Express*, said it was 'a very ordinary rock number with nothing especially exciting or catchy about it.' A few months later, he was complaining that Chuck Berry 'already sounds old fashioned'.

Fordyce wanted to chuck Berry away and, to the uninitiated, the records did sound similar. Chuck fused his light voice with his piercing electric guitar – and there is little else happening. There's a madcap piano solo on 'Sweet Little Sixteen' but, by and large, the piano, drums, bass and sometimes sax were very definitely the backup instruments.

Chuck's main strength was in his lyrics, and 'Sweet Little Sixteen' is a perfect example. His love of America and its place names runs through his songs. Consider the opening lines of 'Sweet Little Sixteen', and the whole of 'Back In The USA' and 'The Promised Land'. Unlike in the rock'n'roll nonsense songs, Chuck dealt lovingly with the teenage preoccupations: dating, partying, driving. He described brushes with authority, whether it be parents, teachers or the police. Although Chuck was over 30 years old, white American kids could identify with the lyrics, and he wasn't mocking them like the Coasters.

'Sweet Little Sixteen' describes the paradox of growing up in America: a raver one minute, in class the next. Chuck dealt with the innocence of youth and the song was inspired by an eight-year-old autograph hunter, who was more interested in collecting signatures than watching the package show. 'She came out ahead,' said Chuck, 'because she had recorded evidence of having met the various artists.'

Chuck was – is – a distinctive live performer with his rolling eyes, crimpy hair, pencil-thin moustache and his Duck Walk, which he had developed to hide the wrinkles in his suit. Catch him in *Jazz On A Summer's Day* where he sings 'Sweet Little Sixteen' backed by jazz musician Jack Teagarden.

But Chuck Berry had the 'grown-up blues'. He was jailed for using a white girl 'for immoral purposes' and although he could have written vignettes about prison life, he denied he had done time and parodied his earlier work with 'Dear Dad' and 'Lonely Schooldays'. While Chuck was inside, his songs were recorded by others. Jerry Lee Lewis made the UK charts with 'Sweet Little Sixteen' in 1962, and Brian Wilson rewrote the song as 'Surfin' USA'. Both the Beatles and the Rolling Stones sang his praises – and his songs – and Chuck had UK hits with 'Memphis, Tennessee' and 'No Particular Place To Go'.

In 1972 Chuck Berry had a UK Number 1, but with a risqué novelty, 'My Ding-A-Ling'. Commentators said that it was not representative, but in a way it was. Chuck has been arrested for placing cameras in the ladies' toilets at his restaurant, and a porno video with his ding-a-ling on display is on sale in Europe. Its title: *Sweet Little Sexteen*. If Chuck put the same energy into his rock'n'roll shows, nobody would complain. As it is, he gets his money in advance, tells a scratch band that they're playing 'Chuck Berry songs', does his contracted 60 minutes and goes home. The fact that he is still rocking is to be applauded, although it's odd to hear a 70-year-old extolling the virtues of someone who is sweet little sixteen.

First released:	1958
Highest UK chart position:	16
Highest US chart position:	2

I n 1997, a controversial new play called *Scouse* opened at the Everyman Theatre in Liverpool. It was about Liverpool declaring independence from the rest of the UK; the authorities needed a national anthem for the new country and their choice was 'Ferry Across The Mersey'. That's how it is with Gerry and the Pacemakers. They had their first hits with the knockabout pop of 'How Do You Do It' and 'I Like It', but Gerry is known for the anthems 'You'll Never Walk Alone', from *Carousel*, and 'Ferry Across The Mersey', which he wrote himself.

Gerry and the Pacemakers were the first artists to have Number 1 records with their first three releases. 'I'd have made it four with "I'm The One",' says Gerry Marsden now, 'but the Searchers stayed on top with "Needles And Pins". I kept telling John McNally, "John, will you get off the bloody top?"' Gerry had two further Top 10 hits, both with ballads: 'Don't Let The Sun Catch You Crying', which has been covered by José Feliciano and Rickie Lee Jones, and 'Ferry Across The Mersey', which has done for Liverpool tourism what Scott McKenzie did for San Francisco's.

ferry across the mersey

gerry and the pacemakers

But the title wasn't Gerry's own. 'A film company wanted to make a movie about us and Tony Warren, who had come up with *Coronation Street*, was asked to write it. I was told that the film would be called *Ferry Across The Mersey* and I was asked to write the music.'

Marsden came up with an endearing melody, dripping in nostalgia. The notes may be similar to 'Venus In Blue Jeans' but it doesn't matter. '"Ferry Across The Mersey" is one of my best songs and the mournful quality comes out best when you hear Frankie Goes To Hollywood's version. Their version is great 'cause they do it nice and earthy. That was on the B-side of "Relax", of all records, which was great for me. The other good song that I wrote, "Don't Let The Sun Catch You Crying", was written with my wife Pauline in mind. That was recorded by José Feliciano and his version is a dream. It is absolutely tremendous.'

Gerry and the Pacemakers split up when he went into acting with *Charlie Girl*, and he now performs with a new set of Pacemakers. 'I'm the one who needs the pacemaker,' he jokes. In 1988, Gerry raised funds for the Bradford fire appeal by recording a new version of 'You'll Never Walk Alone', and the following year he did the

same for the Zeebrugge appeal by joining the Christians, Holly Johnson and Paul McCartney for a new version of 'Ferry Across The Mersey'. This time the song went to Number 1.

In 1996, Gerry went on a national tour in a stage musical about his life called (would you believe) *Ferry Across The Mersey*. At the time of writing, he is about to tour the UK with Peter Noone.

Of all the 100 entries in this book, we can guarantee that 'Ferry Across The Mersey' will still be sung in 100 years' time. It captures the whole spirit of Liverpool and, naturally, you can't go on the ferry without hearing it.

Does Gerry get royalties for that? 'I don't know – I've never asked! I go there from time to time and I don't care if they don't pay me. It's so nice that they've adopted it as their song.'

First released:	1964
Highest UK chart position:	8
Highest US chart position:	6

walk on by
dionne warwick

Phil Spector was appalled. As a panellist on TV's *Juke Box Jury*, he had heard Cilla Black's cover version of 'Anyone Who Had A Heart'. Anyone who had ears could tell it was a complete, though inferior, copy of the American original, fumed Spector, demanding a copyright law to protect musical arrangements.

That original Dionne Warwick recording, arranged and produced by co-writer Burt Bacharach, floundered at Number 42 as Cilla made her way to the top. For Dionne, it was a case of look Black in anger. Her next single, 'Walk On By', rush-released by Pye to thwart covers, made the Top 10, but its Number 9 peak position belies the song's classic status. Bacharach wasn't as impassioned as Spector about copycat arrangements, as he worked with Cilla on her 1966 hit, 'Alfie'.

Dionne started her recording career as a backing singer with sister Dee Dee and aunt Cissy Houston (mother of Whitney) in New York City, which in the early 1960s throbbed with creative energy. Black music was growing more sophisticated in the hands of innovative white writer-producers, enriching mainstream pop in the process.

While Leiber and Stoller at Atlantic experimented with strings and Latin beats on Drifters' sessions, Bacharach and David, as staff writers for Scepter Records, were breaking new ground where Rodgers and Hart met rhythm and blues. Compared to the teen-oriented output of younger Brill Building writers, their songs were adult and technically unusual, with words, melodies, harmonies and arrangements skilfully interwoven.

By 1962, when Bacharach and lyricist Hal David began their lengthy association with Dionne Warwick, they were already seasoned songwriters, with hits including 'The Story Of My Life' and 'Magic Moments'. Bacharach was also an accomplished arranger and pianist, touring with Marlene Dietrich. The pair's more complex 1960s compositions provided strong, emotional material for white pop singers such as Gene Pitney and Dusty Springfield, but found their perfect interpreter in Dionne's pure and soulful voice, which was able to ride intricate orchestrations with graceful ease.

Untypically for Bacharach and David, 'Walk On By' was not an original title, as a country 'cheating song' of the same name by Leroy Van Dyke had been a hit in 1962. Nor was it one of David's elongated, often alliterative titles ('Twenty-four Hours From Tulsa' or 'What The World Needs Now Is Love').

Characteristic, however, is the track's sound and structure. The choppy, edgy percussion intro sets up a brisk walking rhythm for the lyric: 'If you see me walking down the street/And I start to cry/Each time we meet/Walk on by'. Dionne's staccato phrasing is punctuated by mellow brass fills, like stabs of melancholy, then joined by a chiming, insistent piano motif and swelling, bitter-sweet strings. The theme is private sorrow, the aftershock of heartbreak: 'Foolish pride/That's all that I have left/So let me hide…'. Towards the climax the tempo quickens, as the R&B girl singers chant 'Don't stop' and the lead vocal launches with fresh intensity into a final plea: 'Now you really gotta go/So walk on by.'

'Walk On By' returned to the charts in 1978 in a Doors-styled arrangement by the Stranglers, who had lived up to their name by taking the song down a dark Tin Pan Alley and mugging it. Isaac Hayes gave it some soulful rapping, while it has also been recorded by the Average White Band, Gloria Gaynor and Aretha Franklin. The 1997 version from Brit Award-winner Gabrielle was faithful to the original, which it outcharted in its first week by entering at Number 7.

The 69-year-old Bacharach has emerged as the father of Easy Listening, although he refutes the tag as a misnomer for his music. Hal David speaks for them both: 'Our songs are easy listening to the extent that people enjoy them but were they easy to write, are they easy to play, are they simplistic? I would say just the opposite.

The songs Burt and I wrote are songs of great emotional impact. They've moved us as we wrote them, I believe they move a lot of people when they hear them.' Quite so. 'Walk On By' is not muzak – it shows that love can be utterly miserable, and how many hit records from 1964 are as deep as that?

First released:	1964
Highest UK chart position:	9
Highest US chart position:	6

In the early 1960s, there was a change in the repertoires to be heard in British folk clubs. Instead of concentrating solely on traditional material, the organizers encouraged performances by visiting American artists. Bob Dylan performed in the London area and Paul Simon, Phil Ochs and Tom Paxton gained experience in UK folk clubs, happily performing for audiences of 100 or 200 people.

Simon had had a grounding in pop music and had even made the US charts with Art Garfunkel in 1957. Billing themselves as Tom and Jerry, they copied the Everly Brothers and cut 'Hey Schoolgirl'. Simon befriended Carole King and they encouraged each other in their songwriting. Two Italian CDs, unbelievably called 'Tom And Jerry's Greatest Hits', present 44 examples of his early work. Simon was capable of copying the dumber pop songs of the day, but there was no conviction in his work or in his voice. 'Wow Cha Cha' sums it up.

homeward bound

simon and garfunkel

Something was stirring inside Simon. He had witnessed Bob Dylan's success with thought-provoking songs like 'The Times They Are A-Changin'' and wanted to do the same. He and Artie cut 'Wednesday Morning 3am', an acoustic album of folk music and a few originals including 'The Sound Of Silence', and Simon came to England in 1965 while Artie continued with his studies.

He based himself in Swiss Cottage, London, sharing quarters with fellow singers Al Stewart and Roy Harper. He fell in love with an English girl, including 'Kathy's Song' on an album recorded here, 'The Paul Simon Songbook'. He went on a tour of one-night stands for £15 a night. 'He turned up on the wrong night to this club in Birmingham,' fellow folkie Harvey Andrews recalls. 'He was allowed to do four songs – "A Church Is Burning", "He Was My Brother", "A Most Peculiar Man" and "The Sound Of Silence" – and by the time he'd finished, I was hanging from the rafters. I'd never heard anything like them before and he was also an astonishing guitarist.'

On Merseyside, he was turned down by the Spinners folk club ('too progressive') and by the Bothy Folk Club in Southport ('He was a conceited man and it came over in his songs. I didn't think he was worth £15 then, and I don't now,' says the organizer Tony Molyneux).

Playwright Willy Russell remembers 'He was very sophisticated and professional. He was doing "an act" which was something that was shunned in English folk clubs because performers used to shamble on and shamble off. Still, the music was terrific.'

Geoff Speed booked him for his club in Widnes. 'While he was staying with me,' says Geoff, 'he was working on a song which turned out to be "Homeward Bound".' The song is an unflattering picture of life on the road and shows that he wanted to return to Kathy in London. 'I don't think it is about Widnes,' says Geoff, 'He was in Birkenhead the night before.'

No doubt, though, that he was sitting in Widnes railway station. 'I took him there twice,' says Geoff. 'Once to go to Granada Television and again when he left for a club in Hull.' There's a commemorative plaque on the station wall, but Simon doubts its worth. 'Widnes? Warrington? Liverpool? What does it matter where I wrote the song?' he told a BBC interviewer in 1996.

Paul cut the tour short because electric instruments had been added to 'The Sound Of Silence' and the record was climbing the US charts. A few weeks later, Simon and Garfunkel had the US Number 1. Perhaps Simon never wanted this to happen, as he was forced to work as a duo and didn't cut another solo record until 1972. His time in Britain's folk clubs stood him in good stead, as he heard Martin Carthy's arrangement of 'Scarborough Fair', which he copied without giving credit. 'Let's just say what he did was not entirely honourable,' says Carthy now.

The break-up of Simon and Garfunkel's partnership was not amicable. Garfunkel released a live album in 1996 with a new version of 'Homeward Bound'. He didn't change the words – with one exception. He sang, 'And all his words come back to me in shades of mediocrity.'

First released:	1966
Highest UK chart position:	9
Highest US chart position:	5

The Kinks came to fame with 'You Really Got Me' and 'All Day And All Of The Night' – songs which, it could be argued, marked the start of heavy metal. However, Ray Davies' songwriting skill was far greater than working up variations of 'Louie, Louie'. He was a cutting commentator on the Swinging Sixties, criticizing what he saw with an affable humour. He satirized Carnaby Street in 'Dedicated Follower Of Fashion', teased trendy partygoers in 'A Well-Respected Man', lampooned the aristocracy in 'Sunny Afternoon' and bravely discussed transvestism in 'Lola'.

waterloo sunset
kinks

His best-crafted composition was 'Waterloo Sunset', from the Kinks' most consistent album, 'Something Else'. The album barely made the Top 40, but the single 'Waterloo Sunset' only missed the top because of Procol Harum's 'A Whiter Shade Of Pale'. Also featured on the album was Dave Davies' solo hit 'Death Of A Clown' and Ray's hilarious schoolboy memory of 'David Watts', later to be updated by the Jam.

The power chords on 'You Really Got Me' mark the Kinks' best-known introduction, but the throbbing start to 'Waterloo Sunset' is just as tempting. As soon as you hear the notes and the exquisite melody, you want to hear the lyrics.

It was Davies' first production for the Kinks and it is perfectly, but sparsely, arranged with piano, bass, drums and guitar and some of the best harmony singing in rock. Ironically, the Kinks released it at a time when psychedelia was in vogue, but that's Ray Davies for you. He steered his own course, and a few singles later he was writing about holidays in Blackpool and presenting his own theory of evolution.

It was never intended to be 'Waterloo Sunset'. Ray Davies had written the song as 'Liverpool Sunset' with the 'dirty old river' being the Mersey. He says, 'The Beatles came up with "Penny Lane" and that was the end of that. I suppose "Waterloo" stuck in my mind because I used to walk over Waterloo Bridge several nights a week on my way to art school.'

The change was an improvement, as he was able to add lines about the people swarming around Waterloo

Underground. The song has Terry meeting Julie, and many have assumed that this is Terence Stamp meeting Julie Christie, although at that time the two film stars had not appeared in a film together. In fact, Ray's brother-in-law, Arthur, had emigrated to Australia and his son was called Terry. In his imagination, Ray Davies had him returning to England and meeting his imaginary dream girl Julie, who symbolized England and may well have been Julie Christie.

For all that, 'Waterloo Sunset', like so many Ray Davies compositions, is a song of isolation. The singer is at home watching the world from his window. He does it so often that he knows that Terry meets Julie every Friday night. He admires their courage in crossing the river, as the song suggests that he does not dare go out.

Just before its release, Ray Davies was involved in a court case with his former management. In court, it was announced that his next single would be 'Waterloo Sunset' and stood every chance of being a hit. 'Will it make me laugh like "A Well-Respected Man"?' asked a barrister. 'It might make you smile if you believe this country has some romance left,' said the enigmatic Davies.

First released:	1967
Highest UK chart position:	2
Highest US chart position:	–

san francisco
(be sure to wear some flowers in your hair)

scott mckenzie

The summer of 1967 was idyllic – the Summer of Love. The protest songs of the previous years were forgotten and everything was 'peace, man, cool, yeah', to quote a Dar Williams song. Hippies today in the UK are New Age travellers, but hippies then were young hedonists who believed in sexual freedom, getting high, psychedelic rock music and an end to war. The hippie anthem, written by John Phillips of the Mamas and the Papas, was perfect: 'If you're going to San Francisco, be sure to wear some flowers in your hair.' He might have added, 'and in your toes as well.'

Scott McKenzie and John Phillips had performed together, singing standards in the Smoothies and folk in the Journeymen. Phillips then formed a hippie vocal group, the Mamas and the Papas, and had hits with 'California Dreamin'' and 'Monday Monday'. Phillips organized the first great pop festival, which took place at Monterey, a sleepy fishing village on the coast of California. They'd had jazz festivals at Monterey, but the residents were very worried about tens of thousands of hippies descending on the town. The song was partly written to comfort the residents, to tell them they had nothing to fear.

John Phillips remembers, 'I wanted a song that would express the feelings of the people coming to the festival. Something that would put them in the right state of mind and tell them to relax. The Olympics appealed to me with laurel wreaths in their hair. I wrote it in an afternoon, did a rough dub that evening, hired the players the next morning, and finished it the next night. Thirty-six hours and it was all done. I'd known Scott since we were teenagers, and his voice was perfect for the song.'

McKenzie agrees. 'My heart was in that song and I didn't have to change my image. I already had a pretty loose life. I was wearing flower shirts, weird flowing robes and kaftans, and we picked flowers the day I recorded the song. One girl gave me a garland of flowers and my friends were sitting there in the lotus position, meditating, while I was recording it.'

The record features noted session musicians Larry Knechtel (piano), Joe Osborne (bass) and Hal Blaine (drums). Blaine's drumming is so steady that some have thought the record featured a prototype drum machine. Handclapping is added by the Mamas and the Papas. For all the spirit of love, the Mamas and the other Papa wished that John Phillips had kept the song for themselves.

The Monterey International Pop Festival was a spectacular success. Appearing after Jimi Hendrix, Otis Redding and the Who, Scott McKenzie closed the festival with 'San Francisco'.

The song became an instant hit and now it is as much an example of social history as an oldie. Despite John Phillips' songwriting, Scott McKenzie had difficulty in following 'San Francisco'. They retained their friendship and McKenzie is now a fully fledged member of the Mamas and the Papas. He gets to sing his hit every night. 'We see ourselves as a travelling rehabilitation centre,' says Scott, 'We save each other's lives. All of us have had encounters with drugs and we need each other's help and support. Timmy Hardin OD'd in Los Angeles. It's a roll of the dice, I guess, as to why I'm walking around and he isn't.'

First released:	1967
Highest UK chart position:	1
Highest US chart position:	4

suzanne

leonard cohen

Contrary to popular belief, there is nothing depressing about Leonard Cohen, not even when he proclaims, 'I've seen the future... it is murder.' As we muddle towards the millennium, Cohen is a fine road companion, his words illuminating the deeper, often darker, subtext of life: 'There's a crack in everything/That's how the light gets in.' Schooled in synagogue, university and the café intellectual milieu of Montreal, Cohen became known in Canada for such poetry books as *The Spicebox Of Earth* (1961) and *Flowers For Hitler* (1964), and the novels *The Favourite Game* (1963) and *Beautiful Losers* (1966). His acute romantic, religious sensibility and gift for ironic observation were assets in his subsequent career as confessional songwriter and performer. Cohen reportedly prepared for this new role by 'listening to old Ray Charles records until they warped'. He recalls, 'I was writing songs rather than a vehicle for poetry... Even when writing a novel, I heard a kind of invisible guitar behind the paragraphs... always a kind of pulse, a drumbeat that seemed to propel an idea forward.'

'Suzanne', the most celebrated of Cohen's early compositions, was written in 1966 and first recorded by Judy Collins on her landmark album 'In My Life', which also included Cohen's 'Dress Rehearsal Rag'. After performing at the Newport Folk Festival, Cohen was signed to Columbia Records in New York, the label which had previously recruited Bob Dylan. His debut release, the haunting 'Songs Of Leonard Cohen', included 'Suzanne', 'So Long Marianne' and 'Hey, That's No Way To Say Goodbye'. A minor US success, the album reached Number 13 in the UK, where he acquired cult status as a world-weary, lugubrious-voiced 'bard of the bedsits'.

And what of 'Suzanne', the girl who takes you down to her place near the river? 'The song was begun and the chord pattern developed before a woman's name entered,' he explains. 'I knew it was a song about Montreal and it seemed to come out of that landscape I loved, which was the harbour and the waterfront and the sailors' church there called Notre Dame de Bon Secours. The song came from that vision, from that view of the river.'

Suzanne is a professional dancer, the wife of the sculptor, Armand Vaillancourt. 'A stunning couple,' says Cohen. 'Every man was in love with Suzanne, but there was no possibility of toiling at her seduction. She invited me to her loft near the St Lawrence River and she served me Constant Comment tea with little bits of orange in it. I touched her perfect body with my mind because there was no other way, under the circumstances.' The song contains enough space for listeners to form their own vision of Suzanne, their own Lady of the Harbour.

The second verse, which has Jesus walking across the harbour, is mystifying to outsiders. Cohen: 'Many people feel that Montreal is the Jerusalem of the North. People brought up here have this sense of a holy city, a city that means a lot to them. I put that verse between the two verses about Suzanne to give it a religious quality, which is the quality of Montreal.'

Leonard Cohen's defining influences are the women, those comforting, mysterious sisters of mercy, who were his muse in the early years. He once wrote: 'I heard of a man/who says words so beautifully/that if he only speaks their name/women give themselves to him'. In *The Judy Collins Songbook*, Judy Collins writes, 'To Leonard, with love, singing "Suzanne" gets me higher than anything.'

First released:	1968
Highest UK chart position:	–
Highest US chart position:	–

galveston

glen campbell

Tom Paxton, on being complimented about his Vietnam song 'Jimmy Newman', said, 'I wish the war had never happened and I hadn't had to write it.' The only good things to come out of the Vietnam war were scores of heartfelt songs, often representing the best work of the songwriters concerned. John Prine touched genius with 'Sam Stone', and there's 'Draft Dodger Rag' (Phil Ochs), 'Waist Deep In The Big Muddy' (Pete Seeger), 'Feel Like I'm Fixin' To Die Rag' (Country Joe and the Fish) and 'I Should Be Proud' (Martha and the Vandellas). Some songwriters wrote obliquely about the conflict, notably Roy Orbison and Bill Dees with 'There Won't Be Many Comin' Home' and Jimmy Webb with 'Galveston'. All things considered, 'Galveston' is the most sensitive and moving song to come out of the war.

Glen Campbell, a Los Angeles session guitarist turned country star, was on a roll with his new songwriter friend, Jimmy Webb. Webb had written his first hit, 'By The Time I Get To Phoenix', and also a song about the working man, 'Wichita Lineman'. Campbell recalls, 'We recorded "Galveston" at the height of the Vietnam war and if you look at the lyrics, it's about a guy sitting in Vietnam, or anywhere else for that matter, away from home fighting. It's about wanting to get back home and now the war is over, I can relate the song to Paul McCartney's "Mull Of Kintyre", which I also do in concert. They have the same feeling about them.'

When asked if it was a Vietnam song, Jimmy Webb said, 'It was about a young American soldier and the only war we were fighting at the time was in Vietnam, so the answer is pretty obvious. I was raised in West Texas and travelled around Texas with my family. The real reason that I chose Galveston was because I wanted a place that was on the sea. I wanted this character to be from the heartland, I didn't want him to be from the west coast, I didn't want him to be from the east coast. He was a character I could identify with.'

Webb included a reference to 'cannons flashing' in the lyric so that it could be argued that it was about the Civil War. The record was a huge hit in the US, topping both the country and the adult contemporary charts. There is a new voice-and-piano version by Jimmy Webb on his 1997 album, 'Ten Easy Pieces'. Webb recalls, 'I went down to Galveston three years later for the big shrimp festival there. It is next door to Louisiana so it has an unusual charisma with cajun overtones.

'I was in a parade going down the street as the guy who wrote "Galveston" and I would say, to be perfectly frank, that there were mixed reviews. I got a couple of things thrown at me but I was in the middle of a politically polarized situation. People didn't know how they felt about that song – is this guy a peacenik or what? They gave me the key to the city, so the majority of them were very happy that someone had taken notice of their town. It's a wonderful place.'

First released:	1969
Highest UK chart position:	14
Highest US chart position:	4

my sweet lord

george harrison

Doo-lang, doo-lang. In March 1963, a New York girl group called the Chiffons went to Number 1 in America with 'He's So Fine'. It wasn't produced by Phil Spector, but he recorded New York girl groups and so must have known the record. In April 1963 'He's So Fine' entered the UK Top 20. The Beatles had a keen interest in American girl groups and they recorded songs by the Shirelles and the Cookies. They knew, and presumably liked, this record.

Flash forward to 1970. The Beatles have split up and George Harrison is making his first solo album. John and Paul had only allowed him a couple of songs an album, so he has a backlog. The result will be rock's first triple album, 'All Things Must Pass'. The record is being produced by one of George's best friends, Phil Spector.

George had been smitten by the Edwin Hawkins Singers' treatment of 'Oh! Happy Day'. He wanted to write an uplifting song himself, and although he was wary about committing himself to a religious belief, he wrote 'My Sweet Lord', at one stage having the backing choir chant 'Hare Krishna'. As George said, 'I wanted to show that Hallelujah and Hare Krishna were the same thing. The song was a simple idea of how to do a Western pop equivalent of a mantra, which repeats holy names over and over again.'

Not that everyone approved. Jerry Lee Lewis' cousin, Rev Jimmy Swaggart, went into print: 'This song glorified a demon-possessed, spiritualist Indian guru with Satan as his master. From that moment, rock music took a turn downward.' Wonder what Rev Jimmy thought of the Rolling Stones' 'Sympathy For The Devil' – and let's not forget that he himself was disgraced for consorting with prostitutes.

George gave the song to Billy Preston and produced his version for Apple, which also featured the Edwin Hawkins Singers. The similarity between 'My Sweet Lord' and 'He's So Fine' is not so marked on this version. When he recorded it himself, the notes for 'My Sweet Lord' and 'He's So Fine' were one and the same. If George hadn't realized, why didn't Phil Spector tell him? Joey Molland of Badfinger, a guitarist on the session, says that the musicians realized the link between the songs, but it was hardly their place to tell their employer

George Harrison was being managed by the American lawyer Allen Klein, who had managed 1960s performers like Sam Cooke and Bobby Vinton. John Lennon was impressed by his knowledge of songs. He would know 'He's So Fine', so why didn't he tell George before it was released?

'My Sweet Lord' was an instant hit, a transatlantic Number 1, but it was more than a record, and as George says, 'It saved many a heroin addict's life.' The connections were made between 'My Sweet Lord' and 'He's So Fine', and Jonathan King recorded 'My Sweet Lord' in the style of 'He's So Fine'. The writer of 'He's So Fine', Ronnie Mack, had died but the song's publisher sued George Harrison. His name? Allen Klein.

Harrison was found guilty of 'unconscious plagiarism' and had to forgo a substantial part of his royalties. Lennon wondered if George had learnt anything from working with him and Paul, but then John was caught for using Chuck Berry's 'You Can't Catch Me' in writing 'Come Together'. You can't catch me, indeed.

The Chiffons revived their career by recording 'My Sweet Lord' and George, retaining his sense of humour, recorded 'This Song'. This song 'don't infringe anyone's copyright', he sings, while Eric Idle comments that it sounds like 'Sugar pie, honey bunch'. 'I still don't understand how the courts aren't filled with similar cases,' reflects George, 'as 99 per cent of popular music is reminiscent of something or other.'

First released:	1970
Highest UK chart position:	1
Highest US chart position:	1

Jethro Tull's fourth album, 'Aqualung', was released in March 1971. A loosely conceptual work, it heralded the direction that the band would take during much of the 1970s, as their music moved away from its blues roots and became more complex and progressive. The album also saw singer/flautist Ian Anderson establish himself as undisputed leader of Jethro Tull by bringing in various key players to replace and expand on the original line-up. The band was developing at an alarming rate. Since their debut for Island in late 1968, 'This Was', an exciting album of blues- and jazz-based material, whose masterly instrumental work was more awesome than many of the songs themselves, Anderson had been slowly building his own empire. Tull had grown out of the Blackpool-based John Evan Blues Band and Lutonians MacGregor's Engine, and shortly after 'This Was' equal-partner guitarist Mick Abrahams left the

aqualung
jethro tull

quartet under mysterious circumstances, just when success seemed theirs.

With Martin Barre in as a replacement, Tull quickly established themselves with two more albums, 'Stand Up' (with its ornate 'pop-up' cover) and 'Benefit', and a brace of excellent chart singles in 'Living In The Past' and 'The Witch's Promise' – cornering an unassailable stellar position for themselves in the progressive rock marketplace. Their appearance at the 1970 Isle of Wight pop festival had been singled out as the highlight of the event by *Melody Maker*, over the likes of Jimi Hendrix and Leonard Cohen.

John Evan had recently been asked to join on piano, and after an autumn tour of the UK another old acquaintance of Anderson's, Jeffrey Hammond-Hammond (he of 'A Song For Jeffrey' fame), had been appointed bassist over the far superior original member Glenn Cornick – rumour had it that Hammond-Hammond was still mastering the rudiments of the instrument when sessions for 'Aqualung' began.

Tull's direction was becoming more and more song-centric, and Anderson's words more bitingly social. He had always shown an ironic, humanistic bent in his lyrics as 'Christmas Song' (the B-side of their 1968 'Love Story' 45) had proved, and 'Aqualung' was a full flowering of his social conscience, the flautist firing off against religion, homelessness and other attendant ills of society. Perhaps taking a leaf out of fellow Blackpool songwriter Roy Harper's book, Anderson crafted a set of sharp polemics aimed at man's injustice to his fellow man.

The clue to the 'Aqualung' character was revealed in the rather pretentious poem included on the back sleeve of the album where, in mock Old Testament tones, Anderson opined 'man formed Aqualung of the dust of the ground… and these lesser men man did cast into the void… and some of them were put apart from their kind… the spirit that did cause man to create his God lived on within all men even with Aqualung, and man saw it not but for Christ's sake, he'd better start looking'. Ostensibly, Aqualung was a down-and-out – this was the era of songs like 'Streets Of London', when the hippie underground came up with the idea of the Shelter organization to care for the increasing groups of homeless people living in the inner cities.

The lyrics to the song were written by Jennie Anderson, Ian's beautiful first wife who worked at the offices of his record label, Chrysalis. The song was a rare collaborative effort and the words were both tough and ambivalent. It was obvious that Anderson saw himself in the character – something that was reinforced by the oil painting by Burton Silverman on the front sleeve that depicted a derelict in a dirty old raincoat, looking

somewhere between Fagin and Anderson himself. (Not three years previously Tull had been living in total squalor themselves as they tried to get the band off the ground.)

Unlike Ralph McTell's 'softly softly' take on down-and-outs, the Andersons harboured both contempt and compassion for the tramp – graphic lines like 'snot running down his nose' were balanced by the singer gently countering, 'Aqualung my friend'. The lyrics built up a powerful image of what it was like to be out on the streets in winter, the steam rising from his breath and the rasping wheezing coming from his disease-wracked body, the sound of which presumably gave Anderson the name of the character in the first place. The arrangement of the tune was equally potent, with acoustic guitar-based interludes and a crushing electric guitar riff from Barre that rammed home the message.

The album was received enthusiastically and became a multi-million-seller, but it also heralded a new phase and after 'Thick As A Brick' (saved by some wonderfully British eccentric humour), Anderson became increasingly pompous. Despite continued popularity, especially in the US, further concept albums like 'Passion Play' and 'Too Old To Rock'n'Roll: Too Young To Die' were pretty dire. However, it's a testament to 'Aqualung's excellence and originality that in 1996 the album was reissued in a 25th anniversary CD pack with bonus tracks.

First released:	1971
Highest UK chart position:	–
Highest US chart position:	–

A long, long time ago, on 3 February 1959, Buddy Holly died in a plane crash. Don McLean was 13 years old, delivering papers. He cried as he put the bad news on the doorstep. Sorry – he might have done, he can't remember. Something touched him deep inside. In years to come, he would call it the day the music died and use the event as the springboard for an elegy to the 1960s and to present his negative critique on contemporary rock. The Doors, the Byrds, the Rolling Stones and Janis Joplin are given short shrift. Or are they? Part of the skill of 'American Pie' is that its lyrics are largely mysterious.

Some images seem straightforward: the jester in a cast can only be Bob Dylan recovering from his motorcycle accident, while Jackflash is Mick Jagger with 'no angel born in hell' being Hell's Angels at Altamont. What about 'the sergeants played a marching tune'? On the face of it, it's a reference to the Beatles and 'Sgt Pepper's Lonely Hearts Club Band', but McLean could be talking about the Vietnam war and the right-wing hit single by Staff Sergeant Barry Sadler, 'The Ballad Of The Green Berets'.

american pie

don mclean

Let's ask him. Well, no, we can't, because McLean, an affable interviewee, never answers direct questions about the song. When asked what 'American Pie' means, he replies, 'It means I don't have to work if I don't want to.' He has conceded the song was not intended to be about the death of music. 'The music never dies, and I was saying that people lack the basic trust to believe that the music will happen again.' In other words, the levee doesn't remain dry.

Because McLean has not commented on the lyrics, numerous critics have sought to explain them. 'American Pie' is rock's equivalent to T.S. Eliot's *The Waste Land* and you can obtain a doctorate by writing on its hidden meaning. Some have thought that the opening verse is about John F. Kennedy rather than Buddy Holly and that 'the widowed bride' is Jackie Kennedy. Then the three men he admires the most become the two assassinated Kennedys and Martin Luther King, which is a long way from imagining they are Buddy Holly, the Big Bopper and Ritchie Valens. Could be: Don McLean won't even say if you're wrong.

'The day the music died' is surely an echo of Holly's own 'That'll be the day when I die', and there are strong clues in McLean's later work. He has revisited the Buddy Holly songbook regularly and had a hit with a revival of 'Everyday', but 'American Pie' – which showed its evergreen quality by reaching Number 12 in the UK on its 1991 reissue – remained the song for which he was best known.

Perhaps McLean was critical of rock music because he was a folksinger. He played banjo and guitar and he worked with Pete Seeger. In 1968 he had been nominated as the Hudson River Troubadour. Perhaps the day the music died was when a dyed-in-the-wool folkie cut an eight-minute single about the death of rock'n'roll.

First released:	1971
Highest UK chart position:	2
Highest US chart position:	1

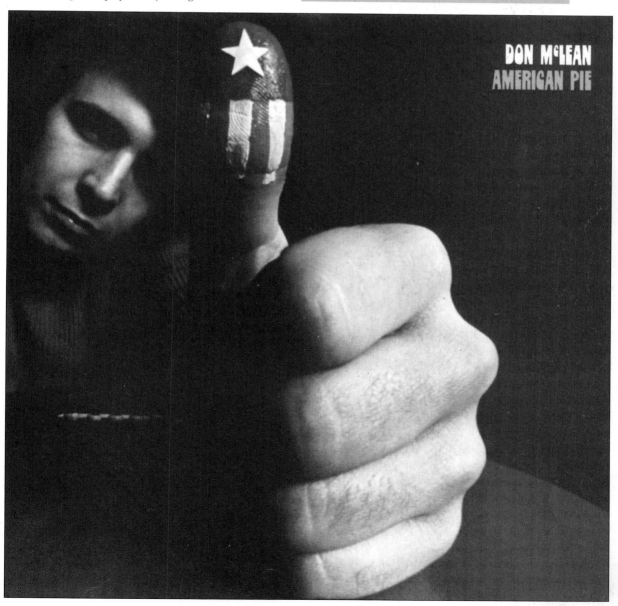

When readers of the *Daily Mirror* and *New Musical Express* were polled in 1992 as to their all-time favourite tracks, they voted into second place a song by a non-existent group from an album that, when released 20 years earlier, had been a resounding flop! There was in reality no Derek, but Eric – Clapton, no less – the master guitarist who had made his mark with the Yardbirds and John Mayall's Bluesbreakers, before finding worldwide fame as one-third of supergroup Cream. After a brief unhappy spell with Blind Faith, the 1970s would see him reject the trappings of stardom, fighting too to rid himself of drug habits he had acquired on the way. The secret was the love of a good woman – but even that tried and tested route was fraught with difficulties, because the object of his affections was his best friend's wife!

Religion was the next option. Like many of his contemporaries, including George Harrison, whose wife Patti was the woman in question, Eric had looked to the East for spiritual guidance. The song took its title from *The Story of Layla And Majnun* by Nizami, a noted twelfth-century Persian poet, and told the story of an ill-starred love affair between the couple of the title. The song pleaded, begged and cajoled as the slide guitar screamed like a train coming off the rails over one of rock's all-time most memorable riffs.

For its singer, the song was 'an emotional experience (inspired by) a woman I felt very deeply about and that turned me down: I had to pour it out in some way… It's the wife-of-my-best-friend scene, and her husband has been writing great songs for years about her and she still left him. She was trying to attract his attention, trying to make him jealous and so she used me, you see, and I fell madly in love with her.' Ironically, Eric and Patti would eventually get it together and marry in 1979.

Alongside Clapton, Derek and the Dominos featured three Americans: keyboards player Bobby Whitlock, bassist Carl Radle and drummer Jim Gordon. All had been members of Delaney and Bonnie and Friends, a loose-knit aggregation with which Clapton had guested. Surprisingly, it was sticksman Gordon who made the biggest creative contribution alongside Clapton, having worked up an instrumental coda on the piano in a break in the session. It earned him a half-share in the composing credit – but that was where his luck ended because, after a dazzling session career and a spell with Traffic, he was jailed for second-degree murder. Two of the other musicians on the session also met sad fates: Carl Radle died in 1980 from a liver infection, while slide guitarist Duane Allman, on loan from the Allman Brothers Band, had a fatal motorcycle accident in 1971.

layla
derek and
the dominos

Clapton of course survived, although his relationship with Patti Harrison did not. Prior to their divorce in 1988, though, he would write another classic for her – 'Wonderful Tonight', a fragile acoustic ballad which couldn't have been further from the emotionally tortured 'Layla'. George Harrison's 'Something' was also inspired by Patti.

Even the hard-bitten Tom Dowd, with a track record of legendary productions as long as your arm, had no doubts as to what had been created. 'When I finished,' he revealed, 'I walked out of the studio and said, "That's the best goddamn record I've made in ten years."' The album had stiffed when first released, but the title song enjoyed somewhat different fortunes. Having peaked at Number 7 first time out, 'Layla' climbed three places higher when reissued exactly ten years on. It was clearly one rock classic that would prove timeless.

First released:	1972
Highest UK chart position:	4
Highest US chart position:	10

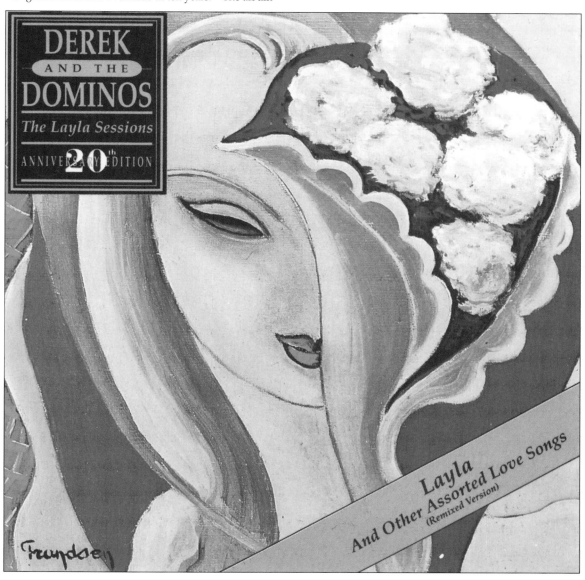

65

candle in the wind

elton john

The most impressive thing about Elton Hercules John is not his personality, nor his voice, nor his music, but his lyrics – or rather, his good sense in having Bernie Taupin write them for him. By and large, Taupin determines the subject matter of the songs, writes the words and presents them to Elton for a tune. Not for nothing did they call a retrospective 'Two Rooms', as they rarely sit down and write something together. Bernie's intricate lyrics are skilfully honed and metred, and it often takes Elton only half an hour to find a suitable melody.

This peculiar way of working says something of the gadfly nature of Elton John's life and the slapdash nature of his creativity. No one is suggesting that we should shoot the piano player, but without Taupin the quality of Elton's work suffers. Elton has collaborated with others, notably Tom Robinson, Gary Osborne and Tim Rice, but the most satisfying results have been with Taupin. That they have the measure of each other is obvious: Bernie once passed him 'The Bitch Is Back'.

In 1973, Elton John had gone to the West Indies for recording sessions, but their relaxed working habits had irritated him and he returned to Strawberry Studios in France with producer Gus Dudgeon, where he had cut two previous albums. He thought he needed some different material, so sat down with a pile of Bernie's lyrics and whizzed through the tunes. 'Jamaica Jerk-off' related to his recent experiences. The results became his best-known album, the double LP set 'Goodbye Yellow Brick Road'. (The album cut reached Number 11 in the UK, but was not released in the States: the chart positions noted refer to a 1987 live recording with the Melbourne Symphony Orchestra.)

Bernie Taupin was on a nostalgia kick, and indeed the very title of the album was inspired by *The Wizard Of Oz*. Bernie wrote about dance halls in Lincolnshire in 'Saturday Night's Alright For Fighting', together with his youthful yearning for the wild west, gangster life and Hollywood. His elegant writing and strong imagery have never been bettered than on his eulogy for Marilyn Monroe, 'Candle In The Wind'.

Marilyn Monroe had been brought up in foster homes, raped as a child, endured loveless marriages and attempted suicide. Her wiggle, her pout and her platinum blonde hair in films like *Bus Stop* and *Some Like It Hot* made her the country's leading sex symbol. Her body was found nude and lifeless in August 1962 and there is still controversy as to whether the 36-year-old star had killed herself or the Kennedys were somehow implicated. This has only heightened the mystique.

Bernie Taupin collected Marilyn Monroe artefacts and he had felt compelled to write about her for some time. 'I wanted to say that it wasn't just a sex thing, that she was someone everybody could fall in love with. I could never come up with the right approach.' The right angle came when Bernie read about the late Janis Joplin being 'a candle in the wind'.

Although Elton loved hearing about glamorous legends, he was also learning that fame could bring despair. 'When I think of Marilyn,' he said, 'I just think of pain. I can't ever imagine her being that happy.' When 'Candle In The Wind' became an international hit, Elton bought Bernie one of Marilyn's dresses as well as a pair of her white satin stilettos.

After the death of Diana, Princess of Wales, in a car accident on 31 August 1997, Elton called Taupin in California suggesting he revise the song's lyrics to produce a eulogy for a woman who, only weeks earlier, had been comforting the singer at the funeral of murdered fashion designer Gianni Versace. Within an hour new lyrics had emerged from the fax machine, and Elton performed the result on 6 September to a TV audience in over 200 countries. He went on to the studio, where Sir George Martin – in his final production role – helped commit to tape a performance that shot to Number 1 and looked set to sell in record quantities.

First released:	1973
Highest UK chart position:	1
Highest US chart position:	1

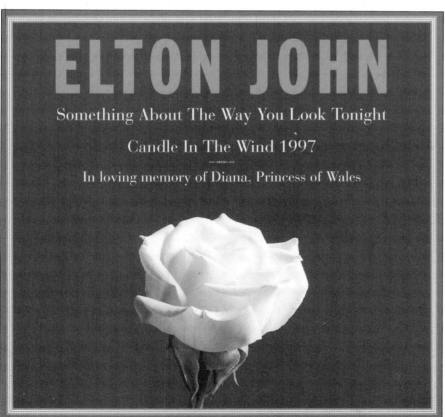

T he Eagles took over from the Beach Boys as the key exponents of California rock, and like them, they became victims of the California lifestyle. At the time of their 1976 album 'Hotel California', the line-up was Don Felder (guitar), Glenn Frey (guitar), Don Henley (drums), Randy Meisner (bass) and Joe Walsh (guitar). Everybody wrote, everybody sang. Felder, Frey and Henley collaborated on the title track and Don Henley took the lead vocal. The album was produced by Bill Szymczyk (pronounced 'Simzik'), whose previously prodigious output slowed right down with the Eagles.

The 'Hotel California' album marked a change in the Eagles' sound, as they wanted to escape from country-rock into something heavier. A new recruit was Joe Walsh from the James Gang, and they spent the best part of a year planning and recording the album in Miami and Los Angeles. Sometimes they stayed in a studio for three whole days at a time.

Felder gave Henley a tape of some of his songs, one of them being 'Hotel California'. He had the basic structure of the song, including its 12-string introduction and the solo at the end. 'I liked it,' said Henley, 'because it was a nice synthesis of cultures. It was a reggae record rhythmically, but musically it was Spanish. It was a Latin-reggae song.' Hence Henley's curious Mexican-tinged vocal.

When they completed the song, the lyrics were about the dissipated lifestyle of southern California, although they also love the place. It was hardly a new idea, and the hotel imagery had been used by Jackson Browne on 'Looking Into You'. Nevertheless, it gave the Eagles a common thread for the album. 'Hotel California' is not a concept album in the style of 'Tommy' or 'Quadrophenia', but it does have a purpose. There's the 'New Kid In Town' adjusting to 'Life In The Fast Lane'. He fears that it has all been 'Wasted Time' and he turns to 'The Last Resort'. As you can check out of Hotel California but can't leave, maybe it has a more universal explanation. Is this a statement about America in bicentennial year?

The song itself was about keeping your health and wits in California and, probably, not taking too much cocaine. Not that the Eagles possessed any great insight. Don Henley told *Crawdaddy* magazine: 'People who live in Beverly Hills who are rich and beautiful have just as

hotel california

eagles

many problems as the people over in East LA.' Well, the people in East LA would probably be delighted to swap their problems any day.

When the album was released, some thought that the Eagles were sending themselves up, especially as the inner cover had them looking glum in the Beverly Hills Hotel. (Ironically, most of their previous album covers had featured skulls.) Joe Walsh said, 'When "Hotel California" came out, we had no idea it would be so big. We'd worked on it for a year, and we hated it because we'd been doing it so long we could play it backwards in our sleep.'

To restore his sanity, Joe Walsh released a solo single, 'Life's Been Good': 'I live in hotels, tear out the walls/I have accountants who pay for it all'. The sentiment could have appeared on 'Hotel California'.

After another tortuously made album, 'The Long Run', and a live set, the Eagles flew away in different directions. Because of the rancour, Don Henley said they would not get back together until 'hell freezes over'. The

Eagles' reunion in 1994 was therefore known as the 'Hell Freezes Over' tour, and the line-up was the same as 'Hotel California' except that Timothy B. Schmit had replaced Randy Meisner. The resulting CD included an acoustic, Latin version of 'Hotel California' – they can check out any time they like, but they can never leave.

First released:	1977
Highest UK chart position:	8
Highest US chart position:	1

killing me softly with his song

roberta flack

American R&B singer Roberta Flack was already an established star when she released 'Killing Me Softly With His Song', with the type of voice that could sing the telephone directory, inject it with pure soul and still see it sell. Her reputation had been made with her memorable interpretation of 'The First Time Ever I Saw Your Face', a sparse, emotion-laden performance of a folk song written by Ewan MacColl, which had topped the charts in the US for six weeks in 1972, the longest spell spent at the chart summit by a female since Gogi Grant in 1956. Indeed, Roberta had quickly established a reputation with her ability to offer existing songs with additional ingredients.

Don McLean was also fast emerging as an exceptional songwriter and performer; he enjoyed two massive US hits with 'American Pie' (a tribute to Buddy Holly) and 'Vincent' (painter Van Gogh), and one of his shows was observed by singer Lori Lieberman. After the show she returned to her songwriters, extolling the virtues of McLean, and asked them to write a song about him. Norman Gimbel and Charles Fox constructed their song around the phrase Lori had used most often in describing McLean, and 'Killing Me Softly With His Song' was the result.

The track duly appeared on her debut album, and Roberta Flack first heard it while listening to the in-flight entertainment on a TWA flight between Los Angeles and New York in 1972. The song would be ideal for her, but she and producer Joel Dorn spent some three months in the studio trying to get it right. They finally achieved the masterpiece they were looking for in February 1973, and the single subsequently hit Number 1 for five weeks in the US. In the UK it became her first Top 10 success, peaking at Number 6.

In March 1974, both single and singer were honoured at the annual Grammy Awards; 'Killing Me Softly' was named Record of the Year and Song of the Year, while Roberta's interpretation was named Best Pop Vocal, Female. In 1996, the song was successfully revived by the Fugees, whose effective drum and bass version topped the UK charts for a total of five weeks and sold over a million copies. According to the group, they had specifically chosen to cover 'Killing Me Softly' to 'bring musicality back to hip-hop'. In this they unquestionably succeeded, but it has to be said that the ingredients to do so were already there, courtesy of Norman Gimbel and Charles Fox.

The main characters involved in the creation of the song have since enjoyed varying degrees of success and fortune. Roberta Flack continues to record, although her chart peaks are considerably lower than they were in the 1970s. Don McLean never quite matched the success of 'American Pie' and 'Vincent', while Lori Lieberman, who effectively started the whole ball rolling, must at present be satisfied with a peripheral role in the success of 'Killing Me Softly'. But if her only contribution was to come up with the phrase, then it is one to which Roberta Flack and the Fugees owe a deep debt of gratitude.

First released:	1973
Highest UK chart position:	6
Highest US chart position:	1

biko
peter gabriel

When Peter Gabriel opted out of progressive rock supergroup Genesis in 1975, he left on a creative and commercial high. After years of slogging round the college circuit since their late-1960s formation, they had brought their complex yet stagey brand of rock to its peak with 'The Lamb Lies Down On Broadway', an overblown double concept album that encompassed everything fans loved and critics hated about 1970s 'prog rock'.

But Gabriel now wanted to follow his personal vision, saying 'I will only make the music which I want to make, and will only then go out to sell it in the best possible way I can.' He was aware that differing from the successful formula risked dissipating his hard-earned commercial status, but that clearly didn't matter.

He didn't help by naming each of his first four albums simply 'Peter Gabriel' (fans added the appropriate numerical suffix, critics didn't bother). And it was during the recording of 'Peter Gabriel 3' that an A&R man from Gabriel's US record label Atlantic came over to check progress and promptly dropped him.

That was a big mistake, For, having graduated from pretty pop songs like 'Solsbury Hill' on his first album to adding what he called 'hard edges' on the second, the third album found Gabriel approaching his music from a different perspective, writing from the rhythm first.

'Normally, I approach them with chords and melody and perhaps lyrics; but for this album I had a small electronic drum machine which I used to set up rhythms and on this track there's a "ba ba ba ba ba ba bum – ba ba ba ba ba ba bum". So I would keep that as a consistent, flowing pattern then the song was written around it, and then the lyrics were really developing from that sort of insistent, almost manic quality of that drum box.'

The outstanding track was 'Biko', also released as a single, which paid homage to murdered South African Steve Biko, who in 1968 formed the all-black students' association SASO. His death in police custody in 1977 had provided a focus for protest against the apartheid regime, and Gabriel's song would become a rallying cry in the fight for democratic rule.

'I identify with Steve quite strongly. I think he seemed very able and articulate and an intelligent youth leader. Maybe he could have been a world youth leader rather than just a black African and I was really shocked when I heard that he had been killed. And you know, normally, I am not a political person but this was just something that I did want to write about. I wrote that song, or rather the information, in my book, some three years ago, and when I started getting these sort of African rhythms it seemed appropriate. Then I did a lot of research on him and the song was completed.'

Unusually, bagpipes featured in the instrumentation, something Gabriel admits 'was a risk… But I checked up with some musicologists and finished by learning that the instrument in fact had an oriental origin and not at all northern. Which gave more reason to my un-Scottish conception of the pipes.'

The African influence would prove to be more than a passing bandwagon for Gabriel to jump on. His involvement in the WOMAD (World of Music and Dancing) festivals actually helped to save the annual event from bankruptcy, when in 1982 he reunited with Genesis for a one-off benefit concert that gave it the wherewithal to continue. He later injected his own money to keep the operation afloat. 'They'd done such a fantastic job,' he said in 1993, 'I couldn't let them go down.'

'Biko' also made him an obvious figurehead for Amnesty International, and he was involved in the 1986 Conspiracy of Hope Tour and again in 1988 – the same year he performed 'Biko' at Wembley for Nelson Mandela's 70th Birthday Tribute. Simple Minds, who were also on the bill, were so impressed that they recorded their own version for the following year's 'Belfast Child' EP, while a new live version had in 1987 graced the soundtrack of *Cry Freedom*, the story of South African journalist Donald Woods who was forced to flee the country after attempting to investigate Biko's death.

The Real World Studios and label was Gabriel's way of paying back a cultural debt. 'People quite often see it as just these white colonialists coming along and ripping off these Third World artists, but it's actually quite a real exchange, I think. But there's some responsibility on those of us who do take ideas from elsewhere to help try to promote the sources of the music.'

First released:	**1980**
Highest UK chart position:	**38**
Highest US chart position:	**–**

happy birthday
stevie wonder

Stevie Wonder's 1980 album release 'Hotter Than July was a vital one for its artist; although 'Journey Through The Secret Life Of Plants' had been a Top 10 success on both sides of the Atlantic, it was a comparative commercial failure. This was not altogether surprising, for the album was effectively a soundtrack to a documentary film. That the film flopped (it was subsequently withdrawn in the US and was never aired at all in the UK) meant that any singles lifted from it had to stand or fall on their own merits; songs dedicated to black orchids or other botanical subjects were not exactly what the record-buying public were handing over their hard-earned money for in 1980, so 'Secret Life' had quickly been dismissed.

For the previous 15 years, just about everything Stevie touched had turned to gold, while some had gone on to platinum, so this was one of the first times his commercial abilities had been called into question. 'Hotter Than July' returned him to former glories, with no fewer than four singles hitting the UK Top 10. Just as with labelmate Marvin Gaye, Stevie Wonder often used his albums to tackle issues beyond the normal 'I love you, you love me' subject matter prevalent in most other pop songs.

Stevie confronted racial, social, environmental and political issues in equal abundance. Central to his thinking at that time was the need to honour one of America's leading civil rights campaigners of the 1960s – the late Dr Martin Luther King Jr, assassinated in 1968. There was much to link King and Motown Records: both had been responsible for giving black Americans their pride, a sense of purpose and an identity, and it was fitting that Stevie Wonder, perhaps black music's most important artist of the 1970s, should be campaigning so vigorously to have King honoured in some way. Stevie had reasoned that all Americans should have an opportunity to preserve the assassinated leader's memory – and what better way than to celebrate his birthday (15 January) with a national public holiday, in much the same way that George Washington and Abraham Lincoln were honoured?

The campaign received most publicity when 'Hotter Than July' was released. Although the entire album was dedicated to Martin Luther King Jr, there was one particular track that became the clarion call: 'Happy Birthday'. Wonder played all instruments (piano, Fender Rhodes, vocoder, drums, bass melodian synthesizer and Fairlight synthesizer) and performed the lead vocal, and the track attracted considerable airplay the minute the album was released, in much the same way that 'Isn't She Lovely' had stood out from his 'Songs In The Key Of Life'. Then, Stevie had resisted the temptation to release the cut as a single, reasoning he could not edit it for seven-inch purposes. 'Happy Birthday' could be edited, but Stevie was still resisting the pressure as three other singles found their way into the UK Top 10.

Then, assured that Motown in the UK could take the single all the way to the top of the charts, he gave in and 'Happy Birthday' was readied for release. There had already been considerable airplay for the track from the album, so Motown pressed up promotional 12-inch copies that contained Martin Luther King's epic 'I have a dream' speech for the B-side (a number of King's speeches had been issued by Motown in the US in the 1960s). The single subsequently exploded into the charts, although it stalled at Number 2, held off the top by Shakin' Stevens.

Surprisingly, given the subject matter, the single was not released in the US, where Stevie maintained his campaign with marches on Washington in 1981 and 1982. The campaign finally won through when 15 January 1986 saw the first observance of Martin Luther King Jr's birthday as a US national holiday.

Although a number of states briefly tried to overturn the decision, Stevie refused to perform live dates in those states until observance of Martin Luther King's birthday was national. And although there is little likelihood that any other country will honour King in the same way, the song is played almost every day by radio stations, usually accompanying a list of stars celebrating their birthdays.

First released:	1981
Highest UK chart position:	2
Highest US chart position:	–

The Specials in general, and keyboardist Jerry Dammers in particular, had been the prime motivating force behind the resurgence of interest in ska music in the UK. After forming the Specials in 1977, Dammers had formulated the idea of forming his own label and utilized his art-college background to put together the image of 2 Tone. After initial copies of the debut Specials single 'Gangsters' (a tribute to Prince Buster's 'Al Capone') had sold through a distribution deal with Rough Trade, 2 Tone was eagerly snapped up by Chrysalis and given its own marketing and promotion budget.

Over the next few years, the label would be responsible for giving Madness, Selecter and the Beat their debut releases. The flagship act, however, was always the Specials, and two Number 1 hits ('The Special AKA Live EP' and 'Ghost Town') and five Top 10s with their first seven releases put the Specials at the top of the ska pile.

It was while the group were at their peak that things began to go wrong, with the various members splitting (although Fun Boy Three would evolve from some of the ashes), and by 1982 only Dammers and John Bradbury remained from the original line-up. Their singles were no

nelson mandela

specials

longer automatic entries into the Top 10 either, and two minor hits in two years seemed to spell the end of the Specials as a creative unit. Against such a background, therefore, the return to chart form with 'Nelson Mandela' was a pleasant surprise, but to have done so with a politically motivated single and one which ultimately became a rallying call and anthem was truly astonishing.

A leading member of the African National Congress, Mandela had been imprisoned by the South African authorities for life in 1964. There had been numerous calls for his release over the years, and the easing of the political situation in South Africa in the early 1980s had raised hopes that he would eventually be freed, but by 1984 he still languished in jail. So Dammers penned this song, with its 'free Nelson Mandela' chorus, and as the single made Number 9 on the UK charts, it quickly became a worldwide call for Mandela to be released.

The success of the single prompted Dammers to take his protest further; he formed Artists Against Apartheid and organized Nelson Mandela's 70th Birthday Tribute at Wembley in 1988 and a subsequent tribute concert in 1990. More importantly, Dammers got his wish: Mandela was finally freed by the South African authorities in 1990 after serving 26 years in prison, and later became South African President.

First released:	1984
Highest UK chart position:	9
Highest US chart position:	—

E ver since Jon Landau first wrote his memorable review of Bruce Springsteen which read 'I saw rock and roll's future – and its name is Bruce Springsteen', the music world had been waiting for Bruce to assume his rightful place in rock's hierarchy. As far as his American and British die-hard fans were concerned, he'd done it ever since 'Born To Run' was first released in 1975, but the rest of the world were still reserving judgement.

The double album 'The River' might have been the one, for there was much on it that would later become the staple diet of Bruce's live shows, but that elusive worldwide hit single still wouldn't come. And the following album, 'Nebraska', wasn't going to provide it either, for this was ostensibly an acoustic album.

born in the usa

bruce springsteen

Bruce, or the Boss as his fans referred to him, spent much of 1983 writing songs for his next album. Inspiration came from a variety of sources; Bruce did no live shows at all during the year, spending his time driving across the country in a pick-up truck. And when the album finally emerged in June 1984, it was something of a revelation. It had been preceded by the single 'Dancing In The Dark' in May, an uptempo item that quickly became a popular feature in his live show, especially when he took to inviting a female member of the audience to join him on stage for the closing bars. This track also saw Bruce's first use of a promotional video, with Brian De Palma directing the action.

It was the title track which immediately leapt out from the album – a driving rock number that evoked memories of Vietnam, unemployment and other issues of importance to a disillusioned nation. There were those who missed the message entirely: Chrysler president Lee Iacocca offered $12 million to licence the track for a series of commercials, and it was quoted by President Reagan at a Republican conference! But to the record-buying public this track, perhaps more than any other on the album, exemplified what Bruce Springsteen was all

BORN IN THE U.S.A./BRUCE SPRINGSTEEN

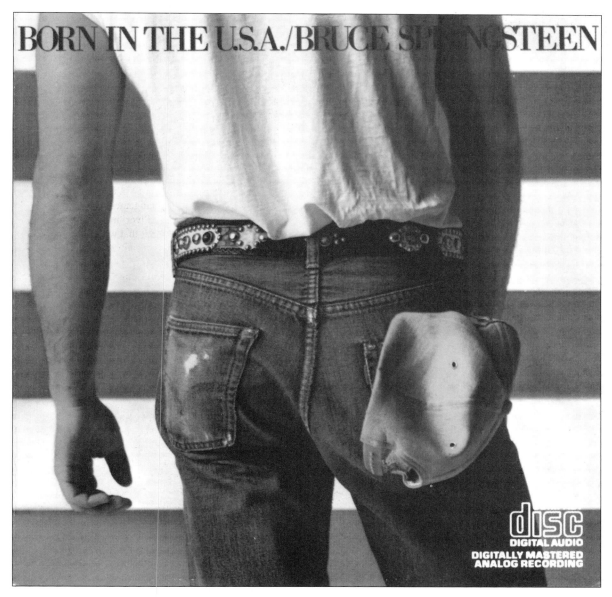

about. Its release as a single in the US saw it surge to Number 9 in January 1985, having already become an instant favourite in his live show.

The accompanying video helped – full of images of an America in decline. It was belatedly released in the UK in July to coincide with the European leg of his Born In The USA tour as a double A-side with 'I'm On Fire', and hit Number 5. Indeed, at the time Bruce could do no wrong, for all seven of his albums were listed on the UK album charts. Rock and roll's future had finally arrived.

First released:	1984
Highest UK chart position:	5
Highest US chart position:	9

sweet child o'mine

guns n'roses

Besides allowing huge benefits, the platform of fame also opens up gigantic crevasses into which the hapless musician might fall. One of stardom's plus points is that artists have the ideal opportunity to express their wishes through the medium of song. However, if stars choose to wear their hearts on their sleeves and express those desires in public, the entire world knows when they end up with egg on their face! And so it was in 1987, when W. Axl Rose of Guns N'Roses put pen to paper in honour of his long-time girlfriend, Erin Everly.

Rose's relationship with Erin, daughter of Don Everly, was an extremely tempestuous one, but the lyrics to 'Sweet Child O'Mine' leave us in no doubt of the affection that he felt for her during their time together. The song opens with 'She's got a smile that it seems to me/Reminds me of childhood memories/Where everything was as fresh as the bright blue sky', but Axl broaches the problem with the line that says, 'I hate to look into those eyes and see an ounce of pain'.

The frontman, who migrated from his home town of Lafayette, Indiana, to Los Angeles to meet his destiny, had been badly beaten by his stepfather in his childhood. As a consequence of this, he now finds himself blighted by an extremely volatile temper. Rose admits to being unable to control his jealousy, and this character deficiency was undoubtedly a major factor in destroying his relationship with Erin. On one particular occasion, at the video shoot for 'It's So Easy', Axl mistakenly thought that a lurking David Bowie was getting a little too friendly with his girl and exploded into a rage, aiming punches his way and then having Bowie thrown off the set. Axl later realized the error of his ways and made his peace with Bowie, but for Erin it was just another in a long line of embarrassments. The pair parted soon afterwards, Erin offering her answer to the song's closing line of 'Where do we go now?'.

Slash, his long-time partner in Guns N'Roses, also testifies how difficult Axl is to get along with. The guitarist is honest about the level of confrontation that has gone on within the band. 'To be a singer or a lead guitar player you have to have a real big ego, they are very temperamental – everyone wants to have their own way!' he admits. 'The biggest fights in this band are between me and Axl, but somewhere along the line we crawl off and apologize politely.' But it's the combination of personalities that makes Guns N'Roses work, and to attempt to change Axl would render him – and them – sterile.

Incidentally, another reason for the popularity of 'Sweet Child O'Mine' is that GN'R's label, Geffen, insisted on releasing the song three times as a single before it finally broke into the UK Top 10. It became a source of frustration. 'Why do they keep doing that? The album is two years old!' wondered puzzled bassist Duff McKagan back in 1989. 'The label don't need our permission, but it seems to us that they're milking the fans. I just hope that we don't get the blame.' The 15 million-plus people who bought the 'Appetite For Destruction' album – from which 'Sweet Child O'Mine' was lifted – clearly didn't worry about such distractions: they simply thought it was a killer tune. And rightly so.

First released:	1988
Highest UK chart position:	6
Highest US chart position:	1

924 148-2

W hen Tori Amos hit Number 1 in early 1997, the dance mix of 'Professional Widow' was light years away from the singer-songwriter style for which she'd become known. A happy accident had taken her to the top after mixer Armand Van Helden took a song from her third album and turned it into a rave anthem. But it was a less happy incident from 1985 that had given her the subject matter for the single that, six years later, would make the rock world first aware of her talents.

me and a gun

tori amos

Tori had relocated to London in early 1991, having seen her first album's worth of songs rejected by a label president singularly unimpressed with 'a female Elton John'. The only course left open to her was to start again, recording at home with boyfriend Eric Rosse, because they had blown their budget.

In the autumn of 1991, a select band of British music journalists were invited to lunch at her record label's offices. Before the festivities began, a mass detour was made to a small flat, literally around the corner, where Tori and Eric had prepared a large pot of herbal tea.

What made the hacks sit up and take notice was not the liquid refreshments but the heady brew that was being served up by this inoffensive-looking girl sitting cross-legged on her piano stool. 'One moment paranoia took hold as the anti-Christ yelled at her from the kitchen,' recalled a bemused writer present, 'the next she was re-living a rape in the back seat of her car.' It was, he concluded, 'a most unsettling *hors d'oeuvre*.'

The song causing such disquiet to the assembled critics was 'Me And A Gun', the lead track of her debut four-song EP. Delivered in those close confines, the effect must indeed have been harrowing. But little was lost on record of a narrative taken from bitter experience.

Billy Bragg, a fellow singer-songwriter, was among those touched by 'Me And A Gun'. 'It's a great song, and she delivers it perfectly,' he enthused, adding: 'That sort of song is all about how you deliver it. Especially live, if you do it right you can silence an audience.' That was exactly what would happen every time she performed it in public — the first occasion being the very day it was written.

'[Rape in her early twenties]'s not something where you just go "Well, get over it". Or "Believe in love and

peace, my child, and it'll all be over." Well, fuck you – that isn't the answer. It's a great thought, OK, but you can go and stick crystals up your butt and let's get on with it. I'm all for love and peace, but that's not the side I work on.

'If somebody would talk about it – or worse, joke about it – I would be ready to kill. That's not healing. It was a very long time after that before I was with anyone again. And it has never been the same as it was before.'

In early 1993, she explained how the movie *Thelma And Louise*, in which Susan Sarandon and Geena Davis blew away a would-be rapist, had helped her come to terms with the incident.

'I had no expression for what happened to me until I saw [the film]. I saw my experience in a new light. All women know what it is to be a victim. If I'm going to relate to people, I can't preach to them. I have to use myself as an example.'

The impact having been made, the four-track EP was slimmed down and the emphasis focused on 'Silent All These Years' – a track far more likely to gain airplay. Both songs featured on her debut album 'Little Earthquakes' – and it was this platinum-seller, not the later 'Boys For Pele', that re-entered the UK album chart after the chart-topping single.

First released:	1991
Highest UK chart position:	–
Highest US chart position:	–

belfast child

simple minds

I t is rare for a traditional song to top the pop charts – and although Jim Kerr didn't recognize the source of the beautiful Irish tune his bass player was playing him, it chimed in perfectly with the feelings of loss and frustration he was experiencing. This was the aftermath of a terrorist bomb at Eniskillen, one of the worst atrocities of the 'Troubles' and one that had claimed the lives of 11 innocent people.

'For a long time I had hoped that we could write a song that would at least acknowledge that something is going on there. In Britain, no one seems to want to ask, or to talk about it. And British bands don't seem to want to write about it – they act as if it's not going on. The fact is that it's about 80 miles from Glasgow to Belfast… so it's a mystery to me how people can just close their eyes to it.'

But Kerr also had a personal grief in mind: his brother's best friend, killed by three knife-wielding youths high on glue. 'The kids who did it had probably never left Glasgow, never seen any countryside, experienced nothing but a broken-down city, living with drunken parents and surrounded by all this urban madness,' Kerr explained. 'I didn't feel, nor did his brother feel, any desire for revenge. There was just a void. And the question – why?'

The musical basis for the song was 'She Moves Through The Fair', a traditional Irish air many musical miles removed from the pomp-rock with which the Scottish group, fronted by Kerr and guitarist Charlie Burchill, had made their name in the post-punk late 1970s. It was also universal enough to bring them their first and only UK chart-topper (they had enjoyed similar US success in 1985 after the typically overblown 'Don't You Forget About Me' was featured in the brat-pack movie *The Breakfast Club*).

Kerr, who had grown up in Glasgow, where sectarianism runs rife to the extent that even football teams Celtic and Rangers attract distinct religious groups, was keen not to take sides, attempting instead 'to see the conflict from the point of view of a person in the middle, who is just at a loss… I was trying to relate not just to the people in Belfast but to people in other places around the world where the same kind of void exists.'

'Belfast Child', produced by Frankie Goes To Hollywood knob-twiddler Trevor Horn, topped the UK chart in February 1989 for two weeks: at 6 minutes and 39 seconds, it became the second-longest single to hold that distinction behind the Beatles' 'Hey Jude' two decades earlier.

The release included 'Mandela Day', a song specially composed and debuted live at a concert celebrating the South African leader's 70th birthday in June 1988, while the 20-minute compact disc version included a cover of

Peter Gabriel's 'Biko', inspired by their joint performance of the song at that self-same event. This inclusion helped 'Belfast Child' become the bestselling single to date on the still relatively new CD format.

In retrospect, 'Belfast Child' marked a change of direction for the band. The album that followed, 'Street Fighting Years', included further songs on a socio-political theme, including a title track dedicated to murdered Chilean poet Victor Jara. Indeed, such was Kerr's principled stand that he refused to play Edinburgh's Murrayfield stadium due to rugby links with South Africa. In 1990 they headlined the Nelson Mandela concert at Wembley Stadium to celebrate his freedom.

To accusations that Simple Minds had 'gone political', Kerr riposted that 'we simply set out to put a date and time on our songs', claiming that 'the very essence of folk music is that you're writing about the people and you're writing about the times.' Certainly, the stance didn't enhance Simple Minds' long-term future, since record sales in the 1990s showed a sharp decline from the pomp-rock years.

Interestingly, it wasn't the last time 'She Moves Through The Fair' would find itself in the public eye – in 1996 it was tackled by 'boy band' Boyzone on their chart-topping 'A Different Beat' album.

First released:	1989
Highest UK chart position:	1
Highest US chart position:	–

Four years before Kurt Cobain stunned the world by taking his own life with a shotgun, a 16-year-old youth from the small US town of Richardsville, Texas, was experiencing similar feelings of depression. In front of the classmates who had been bullying him for the past few months, Jeremy Wade Delle put the barrel of a .347 Magnum pistol into his mouth and pulled the trigger.

The story of Delle's suicide on 8 January 1991 was widely reported in the US at the time, and it touched a nerve in Eddie Vedder, lead singer of Seattle band Pearl Jam. 'Jeremy', a track from the quintet's eponymous 1991 debut album, was borne of the incident, and it also became their third single, going on to sell well over a million copies.

'It's a good story, a kid blew his brains out in front of his English class,' observes Vedder. 'That kind of thing probably happens once a week in America. It's a by-product of the American fascination, or rather perversion, with guns. Parental neglect and abuse is the source of many problems. Childhood is such a critical time of a child's development. Many of the things that happen to you as a child resurface in later life.'

Doubtless there's an autobiographical element in Vedder's concern for Jeremy. Pearl Jam have since gone on to become one of the world's most successful rock acts, but as their fame has spread, so Vedder has chosen to withdraw into a cocoon of his own making. Rarely interviewed, the increasingly sensitive frontman shuns the spotlight, maintaining that his band's music expresses everything that they have to say. Whether this is due to insecurity or to a more fundamental dislike of the media is unclear (one would suspect the latter), but Vedder has gone on record expressing his sympathy for yet another American youth who was unable to find a place for himself in this increasingly complex society of ours.

'Don't get me wrong, I wouldn't want to do it myself or anything,' muses the man behind the lyrics, 'but there's a sense of – and I frighten myself by relating to it so much – a sense of "Fuck it, if I'm going down, and it's not my fault and I did everything I fucking could, and I worked with these hands and I didn't do drugs, if I'm out of here, then I'm taking a few people with me…"' These feelings of anger and despair are best summed up when Vedder croons: 'Jeremy spoke in class today/

jeremy

pearl jam

Clearly I remember/Picking on the boy/Seemed a harmless little fuck/But we unleashed a lion.'

'Jeremy' earned Pearl Jam a gold disc and set them on the path to worldwide superstardom – in 1992 they even managed to outsell Nirvana, much to Cobain's frustration. The tune also demonstrated the caring side to their personalities. That didn't stop certain people accusing them of cashing in on a sad course of events, but the video for 'Jeremy' still scooped no less than four prizes at that year's MTV Awards – despite Vedder's unhappiness with the promo ('It ruined my vision of the song'). Pearl Jam declined to play the tune in question that night, but Eddie Vedder did tell the astonished crowd: 'If it weren't for music, I'd have shot myself.'

First released:	1992
Highest UK chart position:	15
Highest US chart position:	79

under the bridge
red hot chili peppers

When you were younger, did you ever have a favourite hideaway? Anthony Kiedis, vocalist of the Red Hot Chili Peppers, certainly did, and many years later he chose to tell the world all about it. 'Under The Bridge', a beautifully melancholy track from RHCP's 1991 'Blood Sugar Sex Magik' album, was written about an area in the poorer suburbs of Los Angeles where prostitutes, lowlife, gang members and winos would congregate and the city's heroin dealers would sell their wares.

Kiedis and Peppers guitarist Hillel Slovak, then both junkies themselves, were fascinated with the place and would visit it regularly, often being so desperate for the narcotics they scored that they would shoot up on the spot. As the song tells us: 'Under the bridge downtown, is where I drew some blood/Under the bridge downtown, I could not get enough.'

The pair were pretty blatant about their illegal habits, but as Anthony once observed: 'I became so familiar with the nature of addiction that I knew Hillel was in as deep as me, he was just more in denial. Hillel thought he had power over the dark side.' Both on and off stage, the Chili Peppers have earned something of a full-on reputation as dudes who, if their song titles are to be believed, go around killing coyotes or throwing a party on your pussy. It was ironic, therefore, that 'Under The Bridge' would be the song to expose them to a whole new audience. A summery ballad that sounded super-cool on the radio, but how many people took the time to listen to the lyrics?

Lyrically, 'Under The Bridge' conveys that sense of isolation which only the junkie can feel. 'Sometimes I feel like I don't have a partner/ Sometimes I feel like my only friend/Is the city I live in, the City of Angels', Kiedis mournfully proclaims at the tune's start. And who can blame him? For, three years earlier, his shared addiction to heroin had robbed him of the pal with whom he had passed those lazy afternoons in the shadow of the bridge.

Hillel Slovak finally died an undignified death on 27 June 1988, having lapsed into a coma and lain undiscovered in his apartment for two days. Unbeknown to Slovak, his increasing unreliability had prompted the rest of the band to consider throwing him out. But, tragically, fate was to intervene on their behalf.

Slovak's death provided Kiedis with one almighty wake-up call, and the singer claims to have steered clear of heroin ever since. In fact, recent years have seen him become something of a staunch opponent of narcotics. Although Anthony has yet to clarify the situation, one can only assume that the poignant 'Under The Bridge' was recorded by the new-look Peppers (featuring guitarist John Frusciante) in honour of his absent friend. There's no mistaking the emotion when Kiedis swears: 'I don't ever want to feel/Like I did that day.'

In another bizarre, drug-related twist, the entire 'Blood Sugar Sex Magik' sessions were recorded in the self-same Hollywood mansion where the Beatles were supposed to have experienced their first LSD trips and where Jimi Hendrix had once temporarily resided. One can only hope that 'Under The Bridge' allowed Anthony Kiedis the opportunity to exorcize a few ghosts of his own.

First released:	1992
Highest UK chart position:	26
Highest US chart position:	2

Like so many 1960s groups, Blur began as a shambolic but promising art-school band, originally called Seymour. By 1991, Damon Albarn, Graham Coxon, Alex James and Dave Rowntree had changed their name to Blur and released their debut album, 'Leisure'. Blur, the first hit band to come from Colchester, then made three albums with cheerful songs based around characters in London's East End: 'Modern Life Is Rubbish' (1993), 'Parklife' (1994) and 'The Great Escape' (1995).

These albums epitomize Brit-pop, but Albarn's vocals are 'mockney', a middle-class boy roughing up his diction. Liam Gallagher of Oasis described their songs as 'chimney-sweep music', while brother Noel described them as 'middle-class wankers'. The press made much of the Oasis versus Blur rivalry. Blur won the Battle of the Number 1s with 'Country House' over Oasis' 'Roll With It', although neither band had released their best single and, in terms of worldwide record sales, Oasis were to leave Blur behind.

Blur's best-known album is the 16-track 'Parklife', which sold a million copies in the UK alone and, with a picture of racing greyhounds on the cover, was launched at the track in Walthamstow. The 1995 Brit Awards confirmed Blur's position. They won Best Band, Best Single ('Girls And Boys'), Best Video ('Parklife') and Best

Album ('Parklife'). The album shot to the top with ease and the single, 'Girls And Boys', about the delights of sex-filled package holidays, made Number 8. The title track was also released as a single, but it stalled at Number 10. It would surely have gone all the way had they issued the Japanese CD version which barks when you open the cover!

Seriously, though, it's hard to see why 'Parklife' wasn't more successful, but perhaps this was because it featured a narration rather than a sung vocal. The lyric was full of amusing detail and quirky cameos ('John's got brewer's droop') and it was delivered with deadpan irony by Phil Daniels, the cockney star of the mods' classic film, *Quadrophenia*: 'I get up when I want, except on Wednesday when I get rudely awakened by the dustman.'

The jagged guitar chords give the songs a jaunty tempo and the vaudeville chorus, when it comes, is irresistible. It was also the perfect song for the video age – and for the 1990s: the highlight of Phil Daniels' day is feeding the pigeons, so this is also a song about the wasting of lives through unemployment.

Numerous influences can be heard in Blur's work, and 'Parklife' sounds like a cross between Madness and the Kinks. 'Parklife' could have been written by Ray Davies, and Blur and the Kinks have paid tribute to each

parklife

blur

other. The very Britishness of Blur's work is said to have gone against them in America, and partly for this reason their 1997 album 'Blur' is 'Parklife' in reverse – darker, less friendly and more grunge-based. This has detracted from Blur's uniqueness and maybe it wasn't necessary, as the Kinks, with equally English songs, became bigger in the US than in the UK.

Political footnote: Labour MP Ken Livingstone can be heard on the third London album, 'The Great Escape'. Had he made a mistake and thought he was going to feature in an album by Blair?

First released:	1994
Highest UK chart position:	10
Highest US chart position:	–

rock classics

Blues master John Lee Hooker has done more than most to popularize the genre to which he seems to have been born. As to *when* he was born, well that's another part of his mystique. It seems he lied about his age to join the US army, and may well have taken his first bow in 1920, not 1918 as often stated. Although Hooker himself is equally reticent about discussing any of his songs in detail, 'Crawlin' Kingsnake' appears to have come from the repertoire of Tony Hollins, a little-known blues singer and guitarist from Mississippi whom John Lee came across in his youth. It is known that Hollins cut it first in 1941, eight years before John Lee's recording debut; but by the time he committed it to tape again ten years later Hooker had made his own version for Modern Records, and enjoyed considerable success with it. As with many of his songs, he recorded it several times, most notably for Vee Jay in Chicago in 1959, but it was the Modern cut that followed the breakthrough 'Boogie Chillen' and 'Hobo Blues' into the R&B charts, establishing the singer's unique style.

It was one of several songs he learned from Hollins, memorizing each and inevitably adding his own twist, consciously or otherwise, as they emerged later. 'I don't want no paper – my paper is here and here,' he'd say, indicating his ears.

This handing down was traditional in blues circles, and also applied to styles: Hooker freely admitted his debt as a guitarist to stepfather Will Moore, whose pick-less strumming he would develop into an almost orchestral style as heard here. The left hand rarely advanced further than the fifth fret, while the 12-bar count often varied by one or two, and the result was unique to Hooker: only the long-forgotten Tony Hollins could begrudge him a writing credit.

The snake motif has long been associated with sex and magic: Blind Lemon Jefferson's 'That Black Snake Moan', Victoria Spivey's 'Black Snake Blues' and the Memphis Jug Band's 'A Black Woman Is Like A Black Snake' are just three examples of its presence as a recurring theme in blues music. On stage in the 1990s, duetting the song with svelte backing singer Vala Cupp –

crawlin' kingsnake

john lee hooker

nearly half a century his junior – Hooker made the meaning of the song crystal clear. 'I caught you crawling early one Monday morning where the grass was real high,' growled Vala. 'Yes baby yes baby,' came the reply. 'I'm gonna crawl up in bed, wrap all around your pretty body, I'll make you feel good.'

As with several of his trademark songs, Hooker re-cut 'Crawlin' Kingsnake' in the 1990s with superstar accompaniment – in this case Rolling Stone Keith Richards, for the album 'Mr Lucky' (1991). 'I did the number with him. It's me and Keith playing guitar… he's a very lovely person.' This time, it featured real drums and not the Coke bottle-tops Hooker had formerly stuck to the soles of his feet in an attempt to become a one-man band. 'Mr Lucky's Number 3 position gave Hooker a place in the record books for the highest-charting blues album in UK history.

The best-known cover of the song came in 1971 on 'LA Woman', Jim Morrison's last album with the Doors before his mysterious demise. It had been a staple of the Doors' early repertoire that had been resurrected not to fill a gap in the album, but to indicate the 'back to the roots' direction Morrison wanted the band to follow, recent busts and bad publicity having clearly soured his appetite for rock. *Rolling Stone* highlighted it as a key track, much to Morrison's evident satisfaction.

'At last, I'm doing a blues album,' he had sighed during recording sessions, while guitarist Robbie Krieger revealed that 'Jim wanted to do more blues, so that would've been the next step for at least one album, maybe two.' Sadly, the Doors' own Kingsnake slithered into oblivion soon after. Other, less celebrated versions came from Hooker's fellow blues legend Muddy Waters, along with later acolytes Little Charlie and the Nightcats, Rockin' Tabby Thomas and George Thorogood.

First released:	1949
Highest UK chart position:	—
Highest US chart position:	—

rock around the clock

bill haley and his comets

You could argue indefinitely about what was the first rock'n'roll record, but most people would plump for Bill Haley's 'Rock Around The Clock'. Haley is a good choice, of course, but he was recording rock'n'roll long before the song that brought him international fame. He was born in 1925 and worked in the country music field in the 1940s as Yodelling Bill Haley.

In 1951 he did a version of a black R&B song, 'Rocket 88', realized that country music with a beat could appeal to teenagers, and changed the band's name from the corny Saddlemen to the Comets. As Bill Haley and His Comets, they recorded 'Rock The Joint,' and in 1953 they became the first rock'n'roll band to make the US Top 20 with a song on a teenage expression, 'Crazy, Man, Crazy'.

Haley's manager, Jimmy Myers, who was also known as Jimmy DeKnight, had written a song called 'Dance Around The Clock' with his partner, Max Freedman, who was born in 1893 (this is teenage music?). To make it more idiomatic, they changed the title to 'Rock Around The Clock', the rhyme of 'rock' and 'clock' being fortuitous. Myers couldn't persuade the US Essex label that Haley should record 'Rock Around The Clock', so he passed the song to Sunny Dae and the Knights.

When Bill Haley's contract with Essex expired, Myers moved him to US Decca. Their A&R man, Milt Gabler, had worked with Louis Jordan and he sensed the same ingredients of up-tempo songs with streetwise lyrics in Haley. Their first session for Decca was at the Pythian Temple in New York on 12 April 1954, and Marshall Lytle (double bass) comments, 'We only had a three-hour session and two songs to record. We spent two-and-a-half hours recording "Thirteen Women" and we only had 30 minutes left to do "Rock Around The Clock". We did two takes and this is what came out.' 'Thirteen Women' was released as the A-side and 'Rock Around The Clock' was described as a 'novelty foxtrot' on the B-side.

Another Comet, saxophonist Joey D'Ambrosia, recalls the guitar break: 'That's played by Danny Cedrone, who had a group with his brother around Philadelphia. He was a great guitarist and a good friend of ours. About three weeks after we recorded it, Danny fell down some steps and died. He never knew that the record was a hit.'

Haley continued to have hits with dance records – 'Shake, Rattle And Roll', 'Dim, Dim The Lights' and 'Mambo Rock'. Myers then arranged for 'Rock Around The Clock' to be included in a film about teenage rebellion called *The Blackboard Jungle*, starring Glenn Ford. The film was denounced as being degenerate, was removed from the Venice Film Festival and led to Teddy Boy riots in England.

On reissue, 'Rock Around The Clock' topped the US chart for eight weeks and the UK for five. It led to Bill Haley and His Comets starring in their own film, naturally called *Rock Around The Clock*. In Liverpool, over one thousand dancing teenagers were chased for a mile by the police. Lord Boothby said, 'What worries me is that a fourth-rate film with fifth-rate music can pierce the shell of civilization. The sooner this ridiculous film is banned the better.'

Lord Boothby would be pleased to learn that Bill Haley had already had his day. When Haley came to the UK, fans saw him for what he was: chubby, smiling, follically challenged and over 30. Nothing wrong with that, but the kiss-curled man wasn't the right person to lead a youth rebellion, although Elvis was.

Teenagers cast Haley aside as quickly as they had embraced him. He made a few excellent records, notably 'Skinny Minnie', but he became an oldies act. Heavy drinking and paranoia were his downfall, and he died in 1981 at the age of 55. 'Rock Around The Clock' remains a classic record, the Comets themselves are still performing, and as Bill Haley often remarked, 'I started it all. They can't take that away from me.'

First released:	1955
Highest UK chart position:	1
Highest US chart position:	1

blue suede shoes

carl perkins

On paper, there's nothing to 'Blue Suede Shoes'. Just 70 words. Yet those 70 words were brilliantly, if spontaneously, chosen. Blue suede shoes themselves are consigned to oblivion – if indeed they ever were in fashion – but Carl Perkins' song remains the classic song of teenage fashion. With slight amendments, the song could apply to mods, rockers, punks and Bay City Rollers fans.

'Blue Suede Shoes' was not written by a teenage tearaway but by a God-fearing family man. Carl Perkins, who was born in 1932, had established himself as a country musician with his brothers, Jay and Clayton. They liked the way that Elvis had added a beat to 'Blue Moon Of Kentucky' and they went to Memphis to audition for Sam Phillips' Sun label. In November 1955, Phillips sold Elvis Presley's contract to RCA and Carl Perkins would be the first to benefit, because Sun were now able to market their releases nationally.

Another Sun artist, Johnny Cash, told Perkins that, when he was in the US Air Force, the servicemen would line up for pay or for food in their brightly polished footwear and they would be telling their companions, 'Hey, don't step on my shoes'. A few weeks later, while playing at a dance in Jackson, Carl heard a young boy tell a girl not to step on his new suede shoes. As soon as the dance was over, Carl worked on the song, scribbling the lyric on a brown paper bag and completing it at one in the morning. Carl's brown paper bag was reproduced in the booklet for his 1996 CD, 'Go Cat Go!', that phrase also coming from the song.

'Blue Suede Shoes' was recorded on 19 December 1955 and the out-takes can be heard on the boxed set 'Carl Perkins – The Sun Years'. At first Carl says, 'Go boy go' but Sam tells him that it sounds too country and it becomes 'Go cat go'. Similarly, an invitation to 'drink my corn' becomes 'drink my liquor'. Carl never regarded the song as anything but country. '"Blue Suede Shoes" is the most country song that has ever been written. There never was a man who appreciated a pair of shoes like an ole country boy, and them city boys don't drink liquor out of a fruit jar. At the time I wrote it, there was no such thing as rock'n'roll. Somebody up north started calling it that.'

'Blue Suede Shoes' was a rarity, a record that made the Top 5 in the pop, country and R&B charts. It was Sun's first million-seller and it was only kept from the Number 1 position by Elvis Presley's first RCA record, 'Heartbreak Hotel'.

Presley's own version of 'Blue Suede Shoes' has a greater urgency and Scotty Moore's guitar breaks leaned more towards rhythm and blues music. Both versions were issued as singles in the UK, with Elvis making Number 9 and Carl Number 10. Carl didn't mind: he accepted that 'Elvis had the looks on me' and evidence of their friendship can be heard in the famous tapes of the Million Dollar Quartet.

In March 1956, Carl and his musicians were travelling from Newport, Virginia, to New York for *The Perry Como Show*. They hadn't slept for two days and the driver fell asleep at the wheel. Their car hit a truck, killing its driver. All the musicians were injured and Carl sustained a fractured skull and broken shoulder. As a result, Perkins' career lost its momentum and some of his rockabilly standards – 'Boppin' The Blues' and 'Matchbox' – failed to make the charts. He tried to recapture the magic of 'Blue Suede Shoes' by writing 'Pink Pedal Pushers' and 'Pointed Toe Shoes'. The best example is 'Put Your Cat Clothes On'.

Carl Perkins returned to country music and worked with Johnny Cash's roadshow for many years. In the 1960s, the Beatles praised his songwriting and recorded 'Matchbox', 'Honey Don't' and 'Everybody's Trying To Be My Baby'. The friendship continued, as Carl's 1996 CD included duets with Ringo, Paul and George. The album ends with John Lennon leading the Plastic Ono Band through a version of 'Blue Suede Shoes'. John may have been a staunch Elvis fan, but the arrangement is 100 per cent Carl Perkins.

First released:	1956
Highest UK chart position:	10
Highest US chart position:	2

Elvis Presley's father, Vernon, had done time. In 1937, when he was poor and had a family to support, he had increased the amount on a cheque from $4 to $14. Nothing too serious, but if Presley's manager Colonel Parker had leaked the information to a friendly reporter Vernon would have been humiliated. So Tom Parker, who had his own skeletons in the cupboard, had a hold over this man. Elvis' mother, Gladys, had no time for the honorary Colonel, but as long as Vernon backed him, he would have no trouble with Elvis. Imagine the Colonel's delight when Elvis was asked to play a convict in the MGM film *Jailhouse Rock*. Elvis had to do it. He was saying to Vernon, 'Don't you dare step out of line.'

Nowadays it is fashionable to sneer at Elvis Presley's movies. True, he made some dreadful ones – *Paradise Hawaiian Style*, *Roustabout* and *Stay Away Joe* – and the songs were usually worse: 'There's No Room To Rhumba In A Sports Car', 'A Dog's Life' and 'Yoga Is As Yoga Does'. The King of Rock'n'Roll even recorded 'Old MacDonald Had A Farm'. Nevertheless, Elvis did have his celluloid moments and they should have given him an Oscar for *Flaming Star*. The early films are the best. He plays a tough tearaway in *King Creole* and holds his own with Walter Matthau. Best of all is his performance in *Jailhouse Rock*, a vintage rock'n'roll film directed by Richard Thorpe, who had made *The Student Prince* with Mario Lanza.

jailhouse rock

elvis presley

The score, by Jerry Leiber and Mike Stoller, who wrote several of Elvis' hits including 'Hound Dog' and 'Loving You', was perfect, if a little short. The pair wrote the whole thing in a day, surely the most productive day's work in the history of film music. There's the sensuousness of 'Treat Me Nice', the tenderness of 'Young And Beautiful', the anguish of 'I Want To Be Free' and the chirpiness of 'Baby I Don't Care'. Elvis must have liked 'Don't Leave Me Now' as he sings it three times in the film. Nothing, however, competes with the excitement of the title song, which was performed in a dance routine involving cells and convicts. It is the only example of full-blooded Hollywood choreography in any of his films.

The movie contains one classic line. When Elvis tries to kiss Judy Tyler she says, 'How dare you think such cheap tactics would work with me,' to which Elvis replies, 'That ain't tactics, honey, that's just the beast in me.'

The 'Jailhouse Rock' single was a smash hit in the US, topping the pop, country and R&B charts. In the UK, it was the first single to debut at Number 1, a common occurrence today but at the time thought an impossible feat. Elvis is forced to sing at the top of his range and, because it is difficult to perform, few artists have covered it. Besides, who could better Elvis' record, which also features Scotty Moore's power chords and D.J. Fontana's great drumming?

The lyrics, delivered at a thundering pace, are both charming and witty. As a result, 'Jailhouse Rock' has been considered a gay anthem. Number 47 flirts with Number 3 in the lyric – and, as they haven't yet built sexually integrated prisons, it stands to reason that both are male.

The film was a smash hit in America, but Elvis' joy was short-lived. A few days after it came out, Elvis received his draft notice for the US Army. He was enjoying himself too much to want that discipline, but Colonel Parker told him it was his duty. And Vernon also said as much.

First released:	1956
Highest UK chart position:	1
Highest US chart position:	1

Alan Price says '"House Of The Rising Sun" is a Jacobean folk song. It was about a brothel in Soho, and the emigrants took it to America, where it became an Appalachian folk song. Blues singers like Josh White then made it their own. It's come full circle really – from England to America to England, from white to black to white.'

The Animals had been discovered by Mickie Most, a wannabe pop singer who would eventually become a top producer. He'd had some success in South Africa and was the opening act on a UK tour featuring the Everly Brothers, Bo Diddley and Little Richard. When the tour was in Newcastle, he went to a club, heard the hard, rough-sounding Alan Price Rhythm And Blues Combo and determined to record them. Renamed the Animals by UK R&B stalwart Graham Bond, their first single, 'Baby, Let Me Take You Home', made the Top 30.

Bob Dylan had included 'House Of The Rising Sun' on his first album, the acoustic 'Bob Dylan' released in 1962. 'Eric Burdon had heard "House Of The Rising Sun" long before the Dylan version,' Animals' drummer John Steel remembers, 'but it was Dylan's version that inspired us to do it. We followed the same chord sequence and we just made it electric.'

Guitarist Hilton Valentine: 'We recorded an album-and-a-half's worth of material on one night. We ran through it once and Mickie Most said, "We'll record it" and that was it, just one take.'

house of the rising sun

animals

One take was sufficient for Most: 'The stars were in the right place, the planets were in the right place, the wind was blowing in the right direction. I can't take too much credit for "House Of The Rising Sun". I just captured the atmosphere, really.'

John Steel recalls: 'Mickie asked the engineer how long it was. It was four-and-a-half minutes but the engineer said it didn't matter because we'd moved from 78s to 45s. It was the first single to exceed three minutes.'

The song was released with the credit, 'Traditional, arranged Alan Price', and those few words led to rancour within the group. Hilton Valentine: 'Channel 4 interviewed all five Animals separately for *Without Walls* and all of us except Pricey said the same thing. Pricey's name went on there because our manager said there wasn't room for all of us. It was understood that royalties would be shared equally. As soon as Alan got his first royalty cheque, he left the band. He said it was because he didn't like flying but he still could have shared the money out.'

To be fair, Alan Price sees it differently, 'First, I based our version on the Bob Dylan record. I took his chord sequence and I rehearsed the band, so it was my arrangement. I hated flying and I was a nervous wreck and drinking too heavily. The other guys couldn't believe their good luck with all the booze, all the parties and all the women. They'd stopped rehearsing and ruined everything the Animals stood for. I couldn't stand it, to be honest.'

The Animals had further hits and both Eric Burdon and Alan Price have developed successful solo careers. Bassist Chas Chandler managed Jimi Hendrix and Slade. Hilton and John now play in Animals 2 and gave 'House Of The Rising Sun' a new arrangement for a single for Preston North End football club in 1996. Maybe the person who has most cause for complaint is Bob Dylan, but apparently not. John Steel: 'We met Bob in New York and he said he was blown away by our version. That record inspired him to go electric, so we influenced each other on that number.'

First released:	1964
Highest UK chart position:	1
Highest US chart position:	1

mr tambourine man

byrds

By 1965, Bob Dylan was regarded as the king of the protest singers, but it was a title he didn't want. He wrote an album of intense, bitter love songs, 'Another Side Of Bob Dylan', and then, horror of horrors, strapped on an electric guitar and recorded a rock album, 'Bringing It All Back Home'. Or, to be accurate, half a rock album: the second side was still acoustic. The songs were quirky and image-laden, and if Dylan knew what 'Mr Tambourine Man' was about he wasn't telling.

He first recorded 'Mr Tambourine Man' with his old friend, Ramblin' Jack Elliott, but a different version was used on the album. It consisted of four long verses and a cheerful, catchy chorus which marked it out as a potential hit song. The imagery was so colourful that it could have been inspired by hallucinating. Indeed, some American radio stations thought the Tambourine Man was a drugs pusher. To be fair, what else can 'Take me on a trip upon your magic swirlin' ship' mean? And what is the point of having a tambourine player in a band if he doesn't have other duties?

Dylan has said that he was inspired by a huge tambourine being carried into a session by the guitarist Bruce Langhorne. He has denied the drug references; but then you would, wouldn't you? It may take away from your creation if you admit you wrote it while high.

A new band, the Byrds, were impressed with the song and recorded it. Jim (later Roger) McGuinn's voice was described as a cross between Dylan and John Lennon and he may have perfected this deliberately. They added the unforgettable 12-string Rickenbacker guitar and ditched three verses to make a classic three-minute single. It's a shame they didn't record the full song as an album cut – but not to worry, the single effectively launched folk-rock and the Tambourine Man was the Pied Piper for others to follow. The Byrds derived their sound from the Searchers and they responded with the anti-nuclear 'What Have They Done To The Rain?' John McNally of the Searchers says today, 'We have often thought about including "Mr Tambourine Man" in our act because so many people think it is one of our hits.'

The Byrds' record was truer to the spirit of Dylan's music than, say, Peter, Paul and Mary's 'Blowin' In The Wind'. It demonstrated that Dylan's songs could be placed in a rock setting and have commercial success without losing their integrity. Many bands were to have hits with Dylan's songs, notably Manfred Mann, and the Byrds themselves recorded so many that an album was released, 'The Byrds Sing Dylan'. Indeed, they followed 'Mr Tambourine Man' with another Dylan song, 'All I Really Want To Do'. Roger McGuinn has worked with Bob Dylan from time to time, but unfortunately they have not recorded an album together. On the boxed set of the Byrds, they back Dylan on a live version of 'Mr Tambourine Man', recorded at a tribute concert to Roy Orbison.

Looking at the song today, 'Mr Tambourine Man' can be seen as brilliant, innovative songwriting. No one had written a song like that before. Robert Zimmerman denied that he had taken his stage name from Dylan Thomas, but the Welsh bard would have been impressed by the new Dylan's wordplay. As Bruce Springsteen said when he inducted Bob Dylan into the Rock and Roll Hall of Fame, 'Dylan was a revolutionary. The way Elvis freed your body, Bob freed your mind.'

First released:	1965
Highest UK chart position:	1
Highest US chart position:	1

tears of a clown

smokey robinson

The year of 1966 was a difficult one for Smokey Robinson. He and his wife, Claudette, who had originally been with him in the Miracles, desperately wanted a family, but she had given birth to twin girls who had both died shortly after. She became depressed and he wrote a beautiful ballad, 'More Love', to describe his feelings for her. At Christmas, Smokey went into Detroit with another Motown writer, Al Cleveland, to find her a suitable present. 'These are beautiful pearls,' he told the saleslady, 'I hope my wife likes them.' Al said, 'I second that emotion' and another hit song was born.

The day wasn't over yet. Although Smokey wasn't up to it, he felt that, as vice-president of Motown, he should attend the Christmas party. Stevie Wonder was there. Stevie said, 'We need your help, Smokey. Henry Cosby and I have written some music but we can't get the words right. Can you help out?'

Stevie and Henry had recorded the music with a fairground calliope leading the way. Smokey liked the sound very much and, although it was cheerful, he thought a sad lyric was appropriate. 'I've got it,' he said, '"The Tears Of A Clown". It can be about the sadness faced by the clown Pagliacci.' Within a few days, the song was complete. It was hardly original – many songs have used the image of laughing to keep from crying, stemming from Leoncavallo's opera 'I Pagliacci'.

Stevie could have recorded 'The Tears Of A Clown' himself, but it was better suited to Smokey's sweet soul crooning. 'The Tears Of A Clown' was released on the 1967 album 'Smokey Robinson And The Miracles Make It Happen'. Why no one thought it worthy of being a single is a mystery.

Although Smokey Robinson and the Miracles were the first group to be signed to Tamla-Motown, a succession of great records meant little to UK record buyers. In 1969, the UK label manager thought that some key tracks were worth reissuing, and so at long last the Miracles had a Top 20 hit. It was with a four-year-old track, 'The Tracks Of My Tears'. Another crying song, 'The Tears Of A Clown' was released next. It went to Number 1 and was a hit in five other European countries. It was released in the US and became the Miracles' biggest record, selling two million copies.

Smokey Robinson didn't know whether to be happy or sad. He was tired of touring and he had already told the Miracles he was leaving. He was vice-president of Motown and was going to concentrate on administrative matters and writing for other performers.

With the hit, the Miracles could command $25,000 a night, so Smokey decided to stay for another year. As he writes in his autobiography, *Smokey – Inside My Life*, 'I hated it, hated it every time I left the house, hated the cabs and the limos and the planes, hated the hotels and the hotel food, hated the hassles and headaches over equipment and musicians and luggage and soundchecks.'

Smokey penned a soundalike follow-up to 'The Tears Of A Clown' called 'I Don't Blame You At All', which was also a US Top 20 hit. His heart wasn't in it, but the great songs ('Cruisin'' and 'Being With You') returned when he developed a solo career.

The Beatles recorded his greatest composition, 'You Really Got A Hold On Me' and George Harrison wrote a tribute to him, 'Pure Smokey'. 'Now he's been around with those tears of a clown,' sings George, 'I want to thank you, Lord, for giving us pure Smokey.' Amen to that.

First released:	1967
Highest UK chart position:	1
Highest US chart position:	1

Three great records were Number 1 during the Summer of Love in 1967 – 'A Whiter Shade Of Pale', 'All You Need Is Love' and 'San Francisco'. What could be more suitable for someone tripping out on LSD than the image-laden, allegorical words of 'A Whiter Shade Of Pale'? If you want to argue that rock lyrics are poetry, what better place to start? The words were by non-playing lyricist Keith Reid and the music was by vocalist/pianist Gary Brooker with a whiter shade of J.S. Bach. The melody itself is original, but 'Suite No 3 in D Major (Air On A G String)' and 'Sleepers Awake' are certainly inspirations. Possibly this element was enhanced by featuring an organ, which was played by Matthew Fisher. A few weeks earlier Fisher had been playing with Screaming Lord Sutch and the Savages, and was unsure about joining Procol Harum because Sutch provided him with regular employment. He brought a sense of theatre to the group: remember his masked appearance in a cloak on *Top Of The Pops*?

a whiter shade of pale
procol harum

Gary and Keith told Matthew that Procol Harum, named after a cat, was going to be bigger than the Beatles. They had already written 'A Whiter Shade Of Pale' and they could sense it was the single. The title had come from record producer Guy Stevens talking to his tired wife, but Keith Reid prefers to let the lyrics have some mystery. The truth is not plain to see. The words may mean nothing at all, but most likely they refer to someone drunk at a party trying to romance some girl. His mind wanders and the different images come into his head. Matthew Fisher says, 'Keith's attitude is that he writes the words and it's up to the listeners to appreciate them on whatever level they want.'

A university thesis could be written on the significance of 'A Whiter Shade Of Pale'. Why does the singer see vestal virgins, and why are there 16 of them? Is the reference to the miller's tale a nod to Chaucer, and why is it there? Pretentious, *moi*? To quote another of their hit singles, Procol Harum had opened a Pandora's box as bands fell over themselves in an effort to be obscure and, hence, significant.

The single was an international hit and, as the millennium draws closer, it is bound to be high on lists of records of the century. The song has been covered by artists as diverse as Willie Nelson and Annie Lennox, but none of them capture the feeling of the original.

Procol Harum followed 'A Whiter Shade Of Pale' with 'Homburg', which contains the riveting opening line, 'Your multilingual business friend'. And to think they had their origins in the R&B band, the Paramounts. After 'Homburg' they became an album act and although they occasionally made the charts, it was albums like 'A Salty Dog' and 'Broken Barricades' that enhanced their reputation. They broke up in 1977 after an album called 'Something Magic', which wasn't.

Procol Harum re-formed in the 1990s and performed 'A Whiter Shade Of Pale' with an extra, equally impenetrable verse. Gary Brooker had a role in the film of *Evita* and recorded a new version of the song backed by the church organ of St Mary and All Saints Church in rural Surrey.

First released:	1967
Highest UK chart position:	1
Highest US chart position:	5

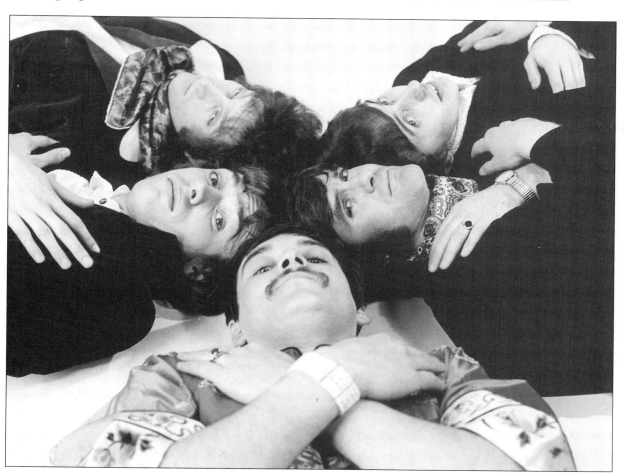

astral weeks
van
morrison

When Van Morrison cut the album 'Astral Weeks' in 1968, he had progressed a long way in a few short months from the angry young man who had fronted Them, the Belfast gypsies who had inspired a host of US garage bands with their feisty R&B. The transitional stage from 'Gloria' to 'Astral Weeks' was a brief solo spell with producer Bert Berns, whom he had followed to the States. But the producer's death and difficulties with the Bang label had left him disillusioned, weary and determined to exert some kind of creative control over his output.

Having cut back to a trio with saxophone/flute player John Payne and upright bassist Tom Kielbania, Morrison entered the studio intending to continue the pared-down, acoustic approach he had been following. Yet once again he found his vision frustrated: his band members were considered too inexperienced to play on the sessions and had to look on from the control room of New York's Century Studios as Morrison mixed with crack jazz session men selected for the task.

Musicians like Connie Kay, drummer with the Modern Jazz Quartet, and bassist Richard Davis, who had worked with Miles Davis, had never heard of Van – and even if they had would likely have been less than impressed. The level of communication in the studio, a watching John Payne remembers, was low: 'Van never talked about anything. He seemed spaced out… in a lot of personal pain.' Ironically, Payne continues, 'the image you have when you listen to the album now is of these guys who are all together and realize they are creating an monumental work of art. But the fact was this was just another session for them.'

The album's eventual title song, 'Astral Weeks' gave Payne the chance to come out from behind the glass when a day's session went so well that an extra, unrehearsed song was cut. He hadn't even brought his flute but, with a borrowed instrument, combined with acoustic guitars, bass and Morrison's often whispered vocal in a special way to make seven minutes of magic.

Although the ending sounds rehearsed, it was the song's first take and unusually had no chord chart for the session musicians to follow. But the recorded version was the only take attempted, and was so successful it named the album. The lack of drums and electric guitars seemed to add to the ethereal quality: percussive effects were limited to the strum of Morrison's acoustic guitar and the repetition of key phrases.

The lyrics themselves were pure stream-of-consciousness imagery, a style which Morrison would adopt as his trademark as the next decade progressed. Years later, when the press asked him why he had started writing mystical songs, Morrison cited 'Astral Weeks' as

'probably the most spiritually lyrical album I've ever done.'

The song itself seemed to revolve around the spiritual search of 'a stranger in this world' looking, in the words of the brief yet insistent chorus, 'to be born again'. Yet, as with the album's other songs, the lyrics mean little without the swirling, ethereal music which adds another vital dimension. 'It's like a transformation song,' said Morrison, 'like transforming energy or going from one source to another with being born again like a rebirth… one of those songs where you can see light at the end of the tunnel. I don't think I can elaborate any more.'

'Astral Weeks' the album was released in November 1968 and, with its lack of standard rock instrumentation, immediately polarized the music press. *New Musical Express* cited him as 'José Feliciano's stand-in,' claiming that only the title track was distinguished. *Rolling Stone*, in contrast, published testimonials from fans, including one who claimed that the album saved their sanity and another who revealed it was a fixture on the tape players of camper vans hitting the hippie trail. Even so, it took many years for sales figures to approach respectability, late-coming fans preferring the commerciality of its successor, 'Moondance', with its collection of shorter, snappier songs.

The mood of the album suggested Morrison had taken the mind-expanding drug LSD, something he later denied. He thought it 'very strange' that 'Astral Weeks' was adopted as an acid classic: 'I didn't need drugs to have experiences. I had always had experiences without drugs and so anything like that would impair them.' Even the cover, with its misty out-of-focus portrait overlaid by waving tree branches, had an ethereal quality.

The whole album resulted from two eight-hour sessions with virtually no overdubs – a fact that gave it a tremendous unity of sound. Although this gave the whole a tranquil, spacey quality, Morrison later told Happy Traum in 1970 that he felt 'the arrangements are too samey… four or five others songs should have had a change of mood.'

The song enjoyed a new lease of life five years after recording as the theme tune of *Slipstream*, an award-winning Canadian film by director David Acona that aimed at exposing corruption in the music business. After his 1960s experiences, it was little wonder Morrison approved of the connection.

First released:	1968
Highest UK chart position:	–
Highest US chart position:	–

Until the mid-1960s, rock albums tended to be a few hit singles with B-sides, wannabe singles and plenty of filler. Then progressive rock bands Pink Floyd and Led Zeppelin cut albums as entities and stubbornly refused to release 45s. They claimed they did not want to be caught in the commercial mainstream of creating short-lived singles, but it was a brilliant marketing ploy. It implied that their work was somehow more durable and that their albums had to be taken as a creative whole.

It meant that record buyers who wanted a particular track had to fork out for a whole LP. Admittedly, Led Zeppelin were forced into releasing a few singles in the States, but if you wanted 'Stairway To Heaven', you had to purchase 'Led Zeppelin IV', which has also been known as 'Runes', 'Four Symbols' and 'Untitled'. Its front cover gave you no idea what it was called – or, indeed, who it was by.

Led Zeppelin were a blues-based, heavy rock band that had emerged from the death throes of the Yardbirds. Their new name, the Mad Dogs, was discarded after Keith Moon said that they would go down 'like a lead balloon'. Robert Plant's overpowering voice was in turn overpowered by Jimmy Page's guitar, and the powerhouse quartet was completed by John Paul Jones on bass and keyboards and John Bonham on drums, who sometimes played with blood-stained hands. 'Led Zeppelin IV' opened with the chaotic 'Black Dog', but the album had more variety than most. Sandy Denny joined them for the folk-based 'Battle Of Evermore'.

The album's *tour de force* was the eight-minute 'Stairway To Heaven', which was written by Plant and Page and fused their electric and acoustic sides together. A parallel can be drawn with Derek and the Dominos' full-length 'Layla'. Led Zeppelin have been accused of writing feeble lyrics, but this one is brimming with

stairway to heaven

led zeppelin

metaphors. It is obscure, but as Robert Plant sings, 'Sometimes words have two meanings.' Sometimes two songs have the same title, too, as they had borrowed the title of a 1960 Neil Sedaka hit. 'Whole Lotta Love' from 'Led Zeppelin II' and 'Stairway To Heaven' have become Led Zeppelin's best-known tracks and heavy metal anthems.

Although much of the album was recorded in Headley Grange, their Hampshire hideaway, 'Stairway' was cut at Island Studios because Page knew it was going to be 'a complex thing to record'. The song breaks with convention by speeding up, which is unheard of today in an era of click tracks. Plant wrote the lyrics while listening to Page teaching Bonham his part, and the result was inspirational.

In the early 1990s, the Australian TV new-wave comedy series *The Money Or The Gun* invited its musical guests to reinterpret 'Stairway To Heaven' in any way they wanted. Rolf Harris had never heard the song before, but he joined in and had a surprise Top 10 single.

First released:	1971
Highest UK chart position:	–
Highest US chart position:	–

willin'
little feat

American songwriters have always had an obsession with the vastness of their home continent and the roads that cross it. Chuck Berry sang about automobiles and lauded 'Route 66', while Bob Dylan put 'Highway 61' firmly on the cultural map. As technology developed apace, the distances were slowly closed by bigger and more elaborate vehicles – as the train fell from favour in post-war US life, so articulated lorries became the only way to ship materials from coast to coast. It was inevitable that the lifestyle of those who drove them would be captured in song, and arguably the greatest paean to the life of the American truck driver was 'Willin''.

The song was written by Lowell George, a denizen of the greater Los Angeles basin who had started his music career in the Factory in 1965–6. His songwriting skills were already burning the critical ears of other contemporary West Coast musos, and it was the Byrds who first brought George's name to worldwide attention when they recorded his 'Truck Stop Girl' on their 1970 double set, 'Untitled'. This was a cautionary tale of a young driver who fell for a waitress at a local roadside greasy spoon and, his mind befuddled with drink and lust, let the rubber hit the road without tying down his load. As George opined, 'it was a terrible thing to see what remained of the rig that poor Danny was in'.

The trucker became a potent symbol of American WASP society in the 1970s, celebrated in movies like Sam Peckinpah's *Convoy* and Steven Spielberg's *The Duel*, and in songs by bands as diverse as Commander Cody and the Grateful Dead.

The Byrds were playing another of his songs – 'Willin'' – live in concert, although their version only ever made their posthumous 1990 boxed set. Ex-Byrds drummer Gene Parsons did, however, record a delightful version of the song on his first solo album, 'Kindling'. George founded Little Feat in late 1969 – the band was named by percussionist Jimmy Carl Black, who had quipped 'little feet' about Lowell's size eights when George was playing with Frank Zappa's Mothers of Invention.

The first line-up of the band comprised Lowell, producer Russ Titelman and legendary session guitarist Ry Cooder – George and Cooder cut a demo of 'Willin'' for a publishing company that Titelman was setting up. When the other two fell by the wayside, Lowell recruited keyboards player Bill Payne (who had tried unsuccessfully to join the Mothers), bass player Roy Estrada (another Zappa escapee) and his pal from Factory days, drummer Richie Hayward.

Little Feat's first, eponymous album in December 1970 was a fabulous slice of Americana, reminiscent of the Band and rooted in the blues. Some honey-sweet country tunes peeked out too, but the highlight was the acoustic 'Willin'' that featured just George and Cooder.

It captured perfectly the romantic life of the trucker – the omnipresent spectre of injury, even death, that rode in the cab, the precarious weather conditions ('I been warped by the rain, driven by the snow'), the roadside belles ('Dallas Alice') who made the long hauls tolerable, and the stimulants ('weed, whites and wine') that helped keep the driver on the road, come hell or high water.

The alliteration of the lines, 'I've been from Tucson to Tutumcari, Tehachapi to Tonopah' evoked the hugeness of the landscape, the rolling plains, the big sky, the Rocky Mountains – a mental checklist of mostly unknown towns ticked off as the truck zigzagged across the interstates, from Arizona to New Mexico and up to California. The song was full of minute observations, from the dodges the trucker might pull to get to his destination on time ('driven the back roads so I wouldn't get weighed') to ways he might earn a little extra 'do re mi' by smuggling drugs or illegal immigrants over the border. And through it all, Lowell praised their courage and their tenacity.

Little Feat recorded a full-on country version of the tune on their second album, the mighty 'Sailin' Shoes', with Sneaky Pete Kleinow on pedal steel guitar, and the song became a perennial favourite in concert, long after the group had assumed a funkier, jazzier style. On the band's last tour of England (where they were always more popular) in summer 1977, the climax of the show was a great singalong version. George sadly died in April 1979 but his work, especially 'Willin'', endures. Recorded by acts as diverse as Sea Train and Linda Ronstadt, the song remains one of the classics of American rock.

First released:	1971
Highest UK chart position:	–
Highest US chart position:	–

David Bowie's numerous chameleon-like changes of character and image throughout his career are legendary. But it is somewhat less well known that even before he had made his commercial breakthrough (in album terms) with 'The Rise And Fall Of Ziggy Stardust And The Spiders From Mars', Bowie had helped relaunch the careers of two other acts – former Velvet Underground frontman Lou Reed and struggling British rockers Mott the Hoople.

'All The Young Dudes' was the song that started the chain reaction. Its success would lead to an album, named after the hit, while the production team of Bowie and guitarist Mick Ronson were also to oversee Reed's second solo album, titled 'Transformer', which would prove to be a creative and commercial landmark. Only then would Bowie turn his attention to the hat-trick with 'Ziggy Stardust'.

all the young dudes

mott the hoople

Mott's and Bowie's paths had crossed after the star-to-be had witnessed them in concert and been impressed by their 'integrity and naive exuberance… I couldn't believe they could command such an enormous following and not be talked about.'

Bowie left a tape of a song, 'Suffragette City', at the studios where they were recording, with a note asking them to ring him with their comments.

As it transpired, the band were on the point of splitting, having run up huge debts and failed to chart with any of their four albums to date. On their return from a Swiss tour in February 1972, Pete Watts called Bowie to thank him for the song and ask if he had a vacancy for a bassist! Bowie: 'They were being led in so many different directions because of general apathy with their management and record company. Everybody was very excited, and because they didn't click immediately it fell away.' A meeting at the offices of Bowie's management, MainMan, saw him sing them another song he thought was just right for them: 'Suffragette City' went back in his pocket, and would reappear on his own forthcoming album.

This one song turned everything round for the band, as Bowie explained. 'Because they were so down I was going to have to contribute a lot of material. Now they're in a wave of optimism, and they've written everything on the album bar one Lou Reed number and the "Dudes" single I did for them.'

MOTT THE HOOPLE

All the Young Dudes

Mott indeed had two gifted writers on board in singer Ian Hunter and guitarist Mick Ralphs. Hunter was perhaps not as accomplished a singer, which is why Reed was coerced into adding a guide vocal to 'Sweet Jane' to give Hunter an insight to the phrasing. Hunter did, however, add his own personal touch to the hit song with his talkover outro: 'Hey there, you with the glasses… I want you.'

The lyric, a tale of youth and disillusionment, was as ambiguous as many of Bowie's classics and, in Ian Hunter's words, was adopted as an anthem 'by the closet gays'. The song had to have a subtle lyric change to pass the BBC's taste arbiters, who wouldn't sanction clothes ripped off from 'Marks and Sparks' (slang for chain store Marks & Spencer).

There was an element of play-acting in the song that links with Bowie's ability to adopt roles. Mott were, after all, cynically swopping denim and flares for 'glam' dress and platform boots. The chorus 'All the Young Dudes, carry the news… Boogaloo Dudes carry the news' was anthemic enough, but the namecheck for Bowie's friend Marc Bolan's then popular band, 'Who needs TV when I got T Rex?', suggested a detachment.

The worldly-wise Hunter had known it was a hit from the word go. 'David was one of the few people who can walk in and there's magic in the room… you feel the guy knows more than you do so you put yourself in his hands. That has never happened before or since with me.' He also recalled that Bowie was the first person to use repeat echo on his voice 'which made me sound infinitely better.'

'Before recording us,' Mick Ralphs recalls, 'they [Bowie and Ronson] came to see the way we performed on stage because they were anxious not to project us different to the way we were.' Ironically, Ronson would fill Ralphs's shoes two years later after Luther Grosvenor, his replacement when he quit to form Bad Company, himself left the ranks.

Bowie would sing the song with Mott on a number of occasions, most notably travelling seven hours from Pittsburgh to Pennsylvania on a rare tour night off, then again at Guildford Civic Hall where he had first met the band – and by all accounts had trembled with nerves at the prospect.

He would later confidently reclaim 'Dudes' for his own stage show, releasing it on 1974's 'David Live' – but Mott's version remains definitive.

First released:	1972
Highest UK chart position:	3
Highest US chart position:	37

Queen, yet another art-school band, played heavy metal with a sense of melody, theatrics and camp humour – what, after all, was the point of their name? Starting in 1974, they had consecutive Top 20 hits with 'Seven Seas Of Rhye', 'Killer Queen' and 'Now I'm Here'. Following a management dispute which left them strapped for cash, they signed with Elton John's manager, John Reid. He threw a lavish party to celebrate the deal.

Freddie Mercury sang the basic framework of a new, grandiose song for the group and their producer, Roy Thomas Baker. 'Now, dears,' he said, 'this is where the opera section comes in.' It was a bit more than that. It took three weeks to record the six-minute 'Bohemian Rhapsody', and the 'Galileo' section involved 180 vocal overdubs. The final version started as a plaintive ballad, merged into multi-tracked operatics and thundered into a heavy rock ending. No one slept while Queen was around.

bohemian rhapsody
queen

'Bo Rhap', as the band called it, was played to John Reid. He told them that they could not possibly release a single that long – no disc jockeys would play it. Untrue, as even longer records ('MacArthur Park' and 'Hey Jude') had been played in the past. He told them it would have to be edited. Queen refused to budge.

Mercury and drummer Roger Taylor passed a copy to Kenny Everett. They told him not to play it on air, knowing full well he would. He was so bowled over that he played it 14 times over the weekend on Capital Radio and the phonelines were jammed with listeners asking about it. Reid relented, and on 31 October 1975 'Bohemian Rhapsody' became the first Queen single to be released in a picture sleeve.

An accompanying video for a hit single is now obligatory, but in 1975 the concept of a promotional film was new. Queen were embarking on a UK tour and they would not be available for television bookings, notably *Top Of The Pops*. They asked Bruce Gowers to direct a promotional film for the record. They were in Elstree rehearsing and they allocated four hours for the film. The shots included bringing the cover of 'Queen II' to life. The film cost £4,500, a tiny amount when you consider that the resulting album, 'A Night At The Opera', had taken four months, involved six recording studios and was billed as the most expensive album of all time.

The video was premiered on *Top Of The Pops* and by the end of November 1975 the record was Number 1, where it stayed for nine weeks. 'A Night At The Opera' also topped the album charts. Some hated their work. American rock critic, Robert Christgau, said they were 'wimpoid royaloid heavyoid android void.' Freddie, of course, loved the idea of combining rock with opera, and in a strange career move he would later record with Montserrat Caballé.

Everyone wanted to know what the song was about, but Freddie wasn't giving much away. 'It's one of those songs which has a fantasy feel about it. People should listen to it, think about it, and make up their own minds as to what it says to them.' He never opened out, except to admit it was about personal relationships. Images of death hang over the lyrics, and if it had been Freddie's last recording critics would have fallen over themselves in analysing its tragic significance.

Freddie Mercury's death shortly before Christmas 1991 set off an enormous sales bonanza. 'Bohemian Rhapsody' topped the charts for another five weeks, with the proceeds going to AIDS charities. Only three records have been at the top for longer. In 1992 the song was featured in the comedy film *Wayne's World*, which indicates that it should not be taken too seriously. The reissued single made Number 2 in the US, with proceeds going to the Magic Johnson Foundation. The flamboyant 'Bo Rhap' regularly tops lists of the best singles of all time, the perfect epitaph to Freddie's mercurial career.

First released:	1975
Highest UK chart position:	1
Highest US chart position:	2

Lynyrd Skynyrd are the band who refused to die, and 'Free Bird' is the personification of their legacy of wild-eyed Southern rock'n'roll. Formed as schoolkids in Jacksonville, Florida, in the early 1970s, they took their name from a sports teacher called Leonard Skinner who would continually complain about the length of their hair, rapidly settling upon a unique sound that incorporated blues, country and simple yet emotionally charged hard rock.

'Free Bird' is the tale of a restless spirit attempting to explain to his sweetheart that he is heading off into the sunset, but explaining that he won't forget her ('If I stay here with you girl, things just couldn't be the same/Cause I'm as free as a bird now/And this bird you cannot change'). The track first appeared on their 1973 debut 'Pronounced Leh-Nerd Skin-Nerd', and soon became the band's calling card. Clocking in at a whopping ten minutes long, 'Free Bird' kicks off with Billy Powell's spectacular lilting keyboard refrain, before segueing into Allen Collins', Steve Gaines' and Gary Rossington's beautiful guitar intro, and building gently into a truly cacophonous triple-guitar conclusion.

'Free Bird' cemented Skynyrd's mushrooming stardom, a reputation that miraculously remained intact when a chartered plane they were travelling in ran out of fuel and crashed into a swamp in Gillsburg, Mississippi on 20 October 1977. The tragedy claimed the lives of singer Ronnie Van Zant, Gaines and his backing vocalist sister Cassie, plus the band's personal manager Dean Kirkpatrick. Lynyrd Skynyrd had been at the very peak of their success, but it was understandably assumed that they would be unable to continue.

However, in 1987 the remaining members got together with Van Zant's brother, Johnny, and realized it was possible. As a mark of respect to Ronnie, initial post-reunion gigs saw 'Free Bird' performed as an instrumental. A solitary spotlight would be trained upon the vacant microphone stand, and Skynyrd would allow audiences the world over to lend their own vocals to the tune in tribute to those who had died. However, in recent years Johnny seems less cagey about treading on his brother's toes, and has been happy to croon those legendary – yet cruelly ironic – opening lines of: 'If I leave here tomorrow/Will you still remember me…'. This

free bird

lynyrd skynyrd

sizzling empathy between band and audience was touchingly documented on the 1996 double live 'Southern Knights' CD.

Over the decades, 'Free Bird' has entered hard rock folklore, now occupying the same 'legendary' territory as Deep Purple's 'Smoke On The Water', Led Zeppelin's 'Whole Lotta Love' and 'Paranoid' by Black Sabbath. With such over-familiarity in mind, you might have suspected that Lynyrd Skynyrd would have developed a love/hate relationship with their most famous song.

'Not at all, we love it as much as ever,' maintains Johnny Van Zant. 'And new people are hearing it all the time, why should we assume that people are tired of "Free Bird" and don't want to hear it anymore? As long as folks go on asking us for it, we'll keep right on playing it.'

First released:	1975
Highest UK chart position:	21
Highest US chart position:	19

wuthering heights

kate bush

Kate Bush, who was born in 1958, wrote 'Man With The Child In His Eyes' when she was only 14. Two years later, she was discovered by Dave Gilmour of Pink Floyd and signed to EMI. In an unprecedented move, they decided not to launch her career straightaway but to wait until her writing, dancing and singing had developed. She studied under Lindsay Kemp, a mime artist and dancer, who had worked with David Bowie on the creation of Ziggy Stardust. Some of her songs from these formative years have appeared in bootleg form as 'The Cathy Demos'.

Like many teenage girls (and Cliff Richard), Kate Bush loved Emily Brontë's tale of uncontrollable passion in the West Riding of Yorkshire, *Wuthering Heights*. Brontë herself was a quiet, solitary person, but who knows what she was hiding below the surface? She let her imagination run riot in *Wuthering Heights*, published in 1847. Kate Bush was inspired by the final page of the novel, in which Cathy goes wandering on the moors looking for her lost and very dead Heathcliff. The images led to her mysterious song 'Wuthering Heights', and she sang 'It's me, it's Cathy, come home again' in a high-pitched, ethereal, demented voice which emphasized Cathy's obsessive love for this man.

The message of the song, as in the book, was that the power of love transcends everything, even death. Although EMI initially wanted the rock-oriented 'James And The Cold Gun' to be the first single, they accepted Kate's choice of 'Wuthering Heights'. In an appropriate move, it was promoted as a romantic single and released in time for Valentine's Day 1978.

Of all the debut singles made by well-known artists, 'Wuthering Heights' may be the most extraordinary. This skilful, well-produced work, which featured Dave Gilmour's guitar and was produced by Andrew Powell, seemed aeons away from the punk explosion. The single went to Number 1 and the resulting LP, 'The Kick Inside', went to Number 3. Not that Kate Bush was too happy, as every article treated her as Britain's new sex symbol: 'The media just promoted me as a female body. It's like I've had to prove that I'm an artist inside a female body.'

Kate delayed her stage debut for a year, but, once again, she made a tremendous impact, a small girl in the presence of elaborate sets. She was the first artist to use a head-mike, which freed her hands for mime. For the music and dancing routine of 'Wuthering Heights', she wore a Victorian nightdress she had bought on a stall in King's Road.

Although Kate Bush was to use other literary sources, notably James Joyce, she never returned to *Wuthering Heights*. There have been seven major film versions of the book, a ballet and an opera, but it did not become a full-scale musical until 1991. Dave Willetts and Lesley Garrett sang Bernard J. Taylor's songs on a CD but it never made the stage. This left the way clear for Cliff Richard's *Heathcliff*. He had been practising his Yorkshire accent in a lavish production, written by John Farrar of the Shadows and Tim Rice. Considering that Sir Cliff is also on EMI, it's fortunate for Kate Bush that the record label didn't want a Heathcliff to complement her Cathy 20 years ago.

First released:	1978
Highest UK chart position:	1
Highest US chart position:	–

Stumbling over a sleeping body on his living-room floor, John Illsley muttered 'Who the hell is this?' He shared an apartment in London with David Knopfler and David had let his English-teacher brother, Mark, stay the night. Within a year, those three individuals, together with drummer Pick Withers, would be on their way to stardom.

Mark Knopfler so dominated Dire Straits that the name just sounds like a pseudonym. It was his voice, his guitar, his songs and effectively his production. True, Muff Winwood produced 'Sultans Of Swing', but it is little different from Mark's original demo.

Mark, who was born in Glasgow and had lived in Newcastle, came to London in the early 1970s. He had played in several bands and by the time his technique was developed, punk music was the rage. They played the same venues and are featured alongside the

sultans of swing

dire straits

Stranglers and the Pirates on an album made at the Hope And Anchor pub in Islington. But Mark's songs and guitar playing were too polished for punk. His music was essentially blues-based, but contained distinctive melodies and sparkling lyrics. Rather like Randy Newman, he wrote in the third person: he was the narrator describing some event. It could be a traditional jazz band called the Sultans of Swing.

Knopfler's song, with its witty, affectionate lyrics, beautifully encapsulates how some people love being part-time musicians: 'living it up for Friday night'. He describes Guitar George who doesn't 'want to make it cry or sing', but Knopfler's own guitar gives the lie to that.

Dire Straits recorded a demo of the song and gave it to rock journalist and broadcaster Charlie Gillett for an opinion. He was so impressed that he played it on his show, *Honky Tonk*, on Radio London the following night. Many industry people listened to his show, and as a result Dire Straits were offered three record deals. They signed to Vertigo and their first album, 'Dire Straits', was produced by Winwood at a total cost of £15,000. It included 'Sultans Of Swing' and also a song of Knopfler's haunts, 'Wild West End'. Many fans visit those places when they come to London.

'Sultans Of Swing' is a great record, with Knopfler's voice a husky cross between Bob Dylan and Lou Reed, and he played the best guitar this side of Jimi Hendrix. His Fender Stratocaster playing was as clean as Hank Marvin's and yet it had a more contemporary edge. He said, 'Everything is based on music that I like to play.'

Dire Straits became a big-selling group, never more so than when CDs were first marketed. For a time, it looked as though the compact disc had been invented for Dire Straits, as they had astronomical sales for their album 'Brothers In Arms'.

But it wasn't brothers in arms at all. Mark Knopfler's demands on the group led to his brother leaving. Now he has put the band behind him as he goes from one session to another, usually in Nashville. He never really wanted to be a superstar: looking back on the lyrics, he envies the Sultans of Swing.

First released:	1979
Highest UK chart position:	8
Highest US chart position:	4

Enormous as he is, the key figure in Meat Loaf isn't Meat Loaf himself. The Incredible Bulk may have an incredible voice, but his songs and his records are arranged by Jim Steinman. They had met in 1974, when Meat Loaf starred in his stage musical *More Than You Deserve* and they appeared together in the *National Lampoon Roadshow*. They found a sympathetic producer in Todd Rundgren and he made the first album, 'Bat Out Of Hell', in 1978. The Gothic cover, like all Meat Loaf albums, conveys the intensity of the imagery and the power of the music. This was an album that had to be played *loud*.

bat out of hell

meat loaf

Steinman had expected equal billing on 'Bat Out Of Hell' and he deserved it. Nothing succeeds like excess, and Steinman's innovation was to take Phil Spector's Wall of Sound and quadruple it, to take Bruce Springsteen's densely packed lyrics and make eight-minute story songs, and to create arrangements with a flair for both theatrics and opera. 'Bat Out Of Hell' was so outlandish, so over the top, that it took the UK by storm and still appeals to new generations of record buyers. It has been on the album charts for the best part of 20 years.

Meat Loaf and Jim Steinman parted company after the second album, 'Dead Ringer', but they needed each other and returned for 'Bat Out Of Hell II – Back Into Hell' in 1993. 'I'd Do Anything For Love (But I Wouldn't Do That)' topped the chart, and then a reissue of the 'Bat Out Of Hell' single did seven places better than the first time round, when it was issued in January 1979.

Much of the instrumentation on the single features Steinman and Rundgren. The lyric reads like a cross between a horror magazine and Bruce Springsteen: 'There's evil in the air and there's thunder in the sky'. In essence, someone is leaving the city, he might have killed someone and he needs to escape. He wants a last night of intense lovemaking with his girlfriend. He sees himself dying after a motorcycle crash, when his heart will leave his body like a bat out of hell. On the other hand, he may be lucky and get back to the girl.

That, with a few variations, is the story of every Meat Loaf record. Every single, every song is a matter of life and death. In song after song, the sweaty fat guy gets the Barbie-doll girl, never better expressed than in Meat Loaf

BAT OUT OF HELL **Meat Loaf** RE-VAMPED

INCLUDES THE CLASSIC "DEAD RINGER FOR LOVE"

and Cher's video for 'Dead Ringer For Love'. His female partner in 'Bat Out Of Hell' is Ellen Foley, later associated with the Clash. 'If you take an average guy and put him in the winner's circle, people like it,' says Mr Loaf.

Through brilliant marketing and well-staged concerts, Meat Loaf is bigger than ever, although not physically as he has slimmed down. 'If they say we're over the top, self-indulgent, bombastic, nothing to do with the times we're living in, they're absolutely right,' Meat told *The Sunday Times*, 'but those aren't negatives. Those are all compliments to us.'

It is surprising that the novelty hasn't worn off for the public, but Steinman fancied a change and went on to produce a musical version of *Whistle Down The Wind* with Andrew Lloyd Webber. Meat Loaf continues touring and, like Randy Newman's 'Davy The Fat Boy', he'll be happy to do his fat boy dance for you.

First released:	1979
Highest UK chart position:	8
Highest US chart position:	—

By the end of the 1970s, very few acts who had had their heyday a decade earlier could hold their heads high in the face of the New Wave. One of these was Neil Young, who entered the 1980s with artistic integrity not merely intact but stoked and blazing. Although he had enjoyed both critical and commercial acclaim with the Buffalo Springfield and as part of Crosby, Stills, Nash and Young, since 1968 Neil had released a series of solo albums that had established him as one of rock's greatest songwriters. Works like 'Everybody Knows This Is Nowhere', 'After The Goldrush' and 'Zuma' had shown that as well as a memorable tunesmith capable of penning both haunting melodies and biting lyrics, Young (often with his backing band Crazy Horse in tow) was also one of the most original, most searing electric guitarists on the planet.

In 1977, as punk rock threatened to blow away all the old dinosaurs that had maintained rock's status quo since the late 1960s, Young was cooling his heels playing the bars of Santa Cruz on the Californian coast with some old mates, the Ducks. After the relative artistic failure of his 'American Stars 'N' Bars' album and an outing with Stills on 'Long May You Run', Neil was readying his three-album retrospective set, 'Decade', and taking stock of his situation.

It was fun being out of the spotlight, playing with old pals Bob Mosley, John Craviotta and Jeff Blackburn, sitting back on his friends' songs to dish out the occasional blinding lead solo, trying out the occasional new tune like 'Comes A Time' or, better still, getting down to dusting off some Chuck Berry covers. There was even time for a little collaborative writing for the first

my my, hey hey
(out of the blue)

neil young

time since Springfield days. But come high summer, the fans, journalists and businessmen crowded into the little town to catch a slice of the action – and, with his cover blown, Neil flew the coop.

It was a strange period for rock – in the UK, Johnny Rotten and the Sex Pistols were shaking the foundations of the establishment, and any self-respecting muso was running for cover. On 16 August 1977 Elvis Presley died a squalid, drug-fuelled death and it seemed as if the world order had changed. For the punks, it was a victory: in their eyes, the middle-aged singer was a bloated banal joke following his seasons in Las Vegas and increasingly uninspired records. For the older generation, who had all followed his rebellious example in the late 1950s and clutched the likes of 'Hound Dog' to their teenage hearts, it was a tragedy.

Unlike many of his peers, Neil fervently embraced the New Wave and collaborated with Akron, Ohio-based avant-punks Devo for a film venture entitled *Human Highway*. Young booked prime San Franciscan punk night spot the Mabuhay Gardens and filmed a sequence there with Devo, performing a new song that had its roots in the Ducks venture, a Young-Blackburn number entitled 'Out Of The Blue'.

In July 1979, Neil released one of his finest albums, 'Rust Never Sleeps' – it proved that while many of his contemporaries were now rapidly stagnating, Young was still at his arresting best. On side two, with Crazy Horse snorting fire from their collective nostrils, Neil delivered a set of some the most scorching rock ever. It showed he could take on the punks at their own game and win – relentless, blistering piledrivers like 'Welfare Mothers' and 'Sedan Delivery' threatened to melt the record to the deck. Side one was mostly acoustic and opened with the aforementioned tune now retitled 'My My, Hey Hey (Out Of The Blue)'.

It acted as a bookend to the album, a reflection on the transience of rock stardom. Young's opinion was plain: it was better to go out in a blaze of glory than to endure a long, slow creative demise. Along the way he ruminated on Presley's death ('the king is gone but not forgotten') and on the deaths of rock'n'roll friends like ex-Crazy Horse guitarist Danny Whitten, and mused on whether the young pretenders of punk would endure. (Ironically, it was 'grunge god' Kurt Cobain of Nirvana who would quote the song's sentiments in his 1994 suicide note.)

Young performed the song with rare passion, and the wailing harmonica gave a doubly bitter-sweet edge to the sentiments. A slightly rearranged version of the same song, 'Hey Hey, My My (Into the Black)', closed the album, powered by the best bar band in the world's engine room and some bristling electric guitar work from Young and Frank Sampedro. The closing lines 'hey hey, my my, rock'n'roll can never die' added a powerful life-affirming coda.

Given Young's erratic career in the 1980s, the song almost became the same kind of albatross around his neck as the immortal line in 'My Generation', 'hope I die before I get old', had become for Pete Townshend, but albums like 'Freedom', 'Weld' and 'Harvest Moon' restored his artistic credentials in the 1990s.

First released:	1979
Highest UK chart position:	–
Highest US chart position:	–

B y 1981, both Queen and David Bowie were firmly established in rock's hierarchy; since making his chart debut in 1969, Bowie had enjoyed two UK Number 1s ('Space Oddity' and 'Ashes To Ashes') and 13 Top 10 hits, while Queen, debuting in 1974, had one chart-topper ('Bohemian Rhapsody') and nine Top 10s to their credit. Up until 1974, the paths of David Bowie and Queen had seldom crossed, although there were many similarities between Bowie and Queen's charismatic lead singer Freddie Mercury, for both were exceptionally fine vocalists and among the truly great live performers of their age.

By July 1981 Bowie was based in Montreux and working in the studio with Giorgio Moroder, recording the vocal for the theme to the film *Cat People*. Working in the same studio were Queen; Bowie and the group got talking and the idea of a collaboration cropped up. The whole project was done in a whirlwind: only one song –

under pressure

queen and david bowie

'Under Pressure' – was actually written and recorded, and there wasn't even a firm plan to release the record. But the end result sounded a sure-fire hit and EMI persuaded the two parties to get the single released.

Roger Taylor claimed it was 'one of the very best things Queen have ever done', while Bowie – although he liked the idea – thought 'it stands up better as a demo. It was done so quickly that some of it [the lyric] makes me cringe a bit.'

As only one song had been recorded there wasn't anything planned for the B-side, so Queen's 'Soul Brother' was added and Queen were given top billing on the A-side as a result. The single, released in the UK in November, was an instant smash, topping the chart for two weeks.

In so doing, the records came tumbling: this was only the second occasion on which two previous UK chart-toppers had combined to scale the charts (the others being Frank and Nancy Sinatra), while Queen became the first act to top the singles, albums (with 'Greatest Hits') and video charts simultaneously in the UK. And while the single fared less well in the US, where it peaked at Number 29, it remained an influential record well beyond its normal chart life – the distinctive guitar and bass riff was later lifted and used to great effect on rapper Vanilla Ice's chart-topping 'Ice Ice Baby'.

First released:	1981
Highest UK chart position:	1
Highest US chart position:	29

relax

frankie goes to hollywood

I f the entries in this book are entirely reliant upon the respective success of the songs as tunes and lyrics, then 'Relax' is the one exception. It was a successful song, a memorable one even, and if you can decipher them there are probably some interesting lyrics in there somewhere. But 'Relax' was more than just a single: for a couple of months at least, it became a catchphrase, a movement and a statement.

Frankie Goes To Hollywood had taken their name from an old newspaper headline concerning singer Frank Sinatra's attempt to become a film star. Fronted by lead vocalists Holly Johnson and Paul Rutherford, the group had first come to prominence thanks to a live performance on the Kid Jensen radio show and a subsequent television appearance on *The Tube*. The latter had included a rough video version of their song 'Relax', which duly attracted considerable attention from numerous record companies – including the ex-Buggle and composer of *The Tube* theme, Trevor Horn, who had just launched his own ZTT (Zang Tuum Tumb) label with journalist Paul Morley. Frankie Goes To Hollywood consequently signed with ZTT in 1983 and work began on knocking 'Relax' into shape for single release.

Although the basic structure of the song already existed, quite how much of the finished product was the work of Trevor Horn and how much the responsibility of Frankie Goes To Hollywood has since become a matter of some debate.

The single was released in November 1983, about the time that the first promotional T-shirts began to appear – the idea of Paul Morley. So while the record began to attract some airplay, so an abundance of 'Frankie Says…' and 'Relax' garments were worn by industry executives. The record would probably have done well under its own steam, but a number of factors then ensured it went all the way to the top of the charts.

Firstly, Radio 1 DJ Mike Read declined to play it for being too risqué, a ban taken up by the rest of the station on 13 January 1984. This only ensured the record received notoriety and aided its selling power. Then a number of remixes began appearing, until by the time the record hit Number 1, there were at least seven different versions on sale. It is reckoned that a number of fans bought all seven.

Just about everything conspired to send the record into folklore; even the original video had to be re-shot because the television stations refused to air it. In the US, the record had to rely on its artistic merits and still managed a credible Number 10 position. It is, of course, the record's UK achievements for which Frankie Goes To Hollywood are best remembered.

When the follow-up, 'Two Tribes' (an even more lavish production than 'Relax' which, ironies of ironies, received its UK radio premiere from Radio 1!), was released and also hit Number 1, 'Relax' surged back up the charts to hit Number 2 (it had already topped the charts for five weeks), making Frankie the first act since John Lennon to hold the top two positions on the charts. Not surprisingly, 'Relax' sold over a million copies in the UK alone, as did 'Two Tribes'. Both singles were subsequently re-released in the 1990s, 'Relax' hitting Number 5 the second time around in 1993.

First released:	1983
Highest UK chart position:	1
Highest US chart position:	10

Given Metallica's almost unrivalled popularity in 1997, it is easy to forget the magnitude of the gamble they had taken when they recruited Bon Jovi producer Bob Rock to oversee their fifth album. The metal community was up in arms when the news broke. After all, this was the man who had worked on BJ's 'Slippery When Wet' and 'New Jersey' albums, as well as Aerosmith's 'Permanent Vacation', 'Sonic Temple' by the Cult and (ulp!) Mötley Crüe's 'Dr Feelgood'. What the hell was somebody like that going to do with a bunch of speed-metal scumbags like Metallica?

The answer was, of course, that he was going to polish off a few rough edges and attempt to take the band on to a new level of success that might perhaps have seemed unlikely, given the sheer uncompromising ferocity of their back catalogue. But while the purists stamped up and down with indignation, there was absolutely no arguing with the results. 'Metallica' (or 'The Black Album' as it is sometimes affectionately known) has now successfully elevated Metallica into the big league occupied by the likes of Guns N'Roses, AC/DC, Kiss and Van Halen, selling somewhere in the region of 15 million copies.

But the track that provided the quartet with their long-overdue breakthrough was its opening cut, 'Enter Sandman'. Lyrically, as with much of Metallica's work, the song was written with a fantasy/horror slant. It brings to life the old wives' tale that sleep is brought to us by a mysterious creature called the Sandman, who drops grains of sand into our eyes and prompts us to drift off into the Land of Nod.

Once there, as anybody who has suffered from nightmares will confirm, we are vulnerable to anything our imagination can inflict upon us. That's why the song utilizes four lines from the traditional Children's Prayer: 'Now I lay me down to sleep/I pray my soul the Lord to keep/If I die before I wake/Pray the Lord my soul to take'. Basically, it's about a visit from the Bogeyman.

'It was triggered by that whole fable thing, but you can take it and deal with it however you want,' says drummer Lars Ulrich. 'I'm not gonna tell people how to react to one of our songs.'

'Enter Sandman' was born on 13 August 1990, in Ulrich's basement, in crude demo form. Metallica being Metallica, they subsequently allowed the rest of the world to hear this instrumental prototype when they released it as a B-side to the official single version a year

enter sandman

metallica

later. From the off it was obvious that they had a huge song on their hands, but it's likely that even Metallica themselves had no idea that 'Enter Sandman' would take them 'off to Never, Never Land' and far beyond.

They may have had some kind of inkling of what was in store when the song was debuted to scenes of unbridled enthusiasm from 10,000 Metallica freaks during an album-listening party at New York's Madison Square Garden. Built around a crunching, mid-paced riff, 'Enter Sandman' boasts a rare accessibility for a hard-rock song. This was formally acknowledged in 1992 when it won a Grammy for Best Heavy Metal Performance, striking a blow for common sense after Metallica had been beaten by old hippies Jethro Tull in the same category the year before!

First released:	1991
Highest UK chart position:	5
Highest US chart position:	16

smells like teen spirit

nirvana

In March 1997, when *Mojo* magazine unveiled the results of its poll on the Top 100 Tracks of the 1990s, the winner was Nirvana with 'Smells Like Teen Spirit'. That highlights its importance, and the fact that the next Nirvana song was at Number 54 indicates its significance over the rest of their catalogue. As a band, Nirvana's career was over almost before it began. Their debut album, 'Bleach', cheaply made for $600, was released in 1989 and became an underground hit. It was powerful rock music that appealed to record buyers who weren't necessarily aware of the distinctions between post-punk, indie, grunge or goth. Nirvana were a heavy metal band with influences such as Neil Young, the Sex Pistols and the Pixies.

'Smells Like Teen Spirit', which owes something to Boston's 1977 smash 'More Than A Feeling', was both the opening track on their 'Nevermind' album and their first UK hit. In 1989 Kurt Cobain was living in a filthy apartment outside Seattle. He and Kathleen Hanna from Bikini Kill decorated its walls with graffiti. She wrote 'Kurt smells like Teen Spirit'. Teen Spirit is an American deodorant, but Kurt did not know this until the record was released.

Its 30-second introduction gives you the flavour of the band: Cobain's power chords, Chris Novoselic's meaty bass and David Grohl's spirited drumming. Cobain's vocal is plaintive and anguished. The disjointed lyric is hard to decipher and anyway was subject to change: 'Load up on guns, bring your friends' became 'Load up on drugs, bring your friends' in concert. The screaming chorus is as memorable as anything in rock, but the answer is nihilistic: 'Oh well, whatever, never mind'. It's the *Trainspotting* culture, but is it any vaguer than the answer being blowing in the wind?

If the song had a purpose, Cobain wasn't telling. He told the *NME*: 'It's about – hey brother, especially sister, throw away the fruit and eat all the rind.' So now you know. He denied any political intent for the song and said it was revolution against the corporate machine – perhaps, in his case, Geffen Records. Kurt Cobain's desperation made him rich. He wrote a song about it, 'I Hate Myself And I Want To Die', which was almost the title of Nirvana's third album, 'In Utero'.

By 1994, Cobain was a heroin addict and fighting to keep his daughter from the social services. Nirvana, who had sold 20 million albums, were in chaos and his marriage to another addict, Courtney Love, was in ruins. There was no stability in his life. In March, he took his fourth overdose within a year. Nirvana were in Rome: they cut short their engagements and Cobain returned to Seattle where he entered a rehab clinic. He discharged himself and six days later, on 5 April, found his own nirvana by blowing his head off with a shotgun. He hated being marketed and had destroyed the face that was on a million T-shirts.

Kurt Cobain was 27 when he died, and very few people over 35 knew who he was. Even fewer had heard his music, but Bernard Levin wrote an obituary: 'This stuff is not just shouting and is even up to making a musical point,' he said. In Levin's view, Cobain was leading people to sanity in the carnage of the modern world. So this is what 'Smells Like Teen Spirit' was saying…

'Smells Like Teen Spirit' has been covered by Tori Amos and parodied by Weird Al Yankovic as 'Smells Like Nirvana'. 'Here we are now, we're Nirvana/Sing distinctly, we don't wanna.' The first bars of 'Smells Like Teen Spirit' were sampled by rappers Credit To The Nation for their single, 'Call It What You Want'.

Ten thousand fans held a vigil in Seattle where Cobain's wife, Courtney Love, read his suicide note. He quoted Neil Young's 'It's better to burn out than to fade away'. Young responded with the tribute, 'Sleeps With Angels'. Like Jim Morrison, Janis Joplin, Jimi Hendrix and even Elvis Presley, it was another unnecessary rock'n'roll death. Chris Novoselic said, 'Kurt had an ethic rooted in the punk-rock way of thinking – no band is special, no player royalty.' Wait for the multi-million dollar film and the new T-shirts.

First released:	1991
Highest UK chart position:	7
Highest US chart position:	6

creep

radiohead

Hailing from Oxford and taking their name from the title of a Talking Heads song on the 'True Stories' LP, Radiohead have become one of the great success stories of the 1990s, an English guitar band that can hold its head up to the likes of REM and U2. 'Creep' was the song that broke them worldwide – one of the great loser anthems of our time that almost came about by accident and whose convoluted genesis from studio to chart-topper was almost as interesting as the song itself.

Like certain other rock icons, notably Kurt Cobain, Radiohead singer Thom E. Yorke saw himself as a misfit, having suffered terribly from a paralyzed left eye as a child and then been subject to bullying at the Abingdon school where he met the other members of the band. Having been signed to Parlophone, the quintet was busy recording their first album, 'Pablo Honey'. The idea was to cut some numbers in a vaguely U2 vein, but once the tape machine was rolling Yorke began strumming a brand-new tune called 'Creep' on his acoustic.

Earlier songs like 'Prove Yourself' had already singled him out as a master of self-loathing, and this latest vignette was no exception. It was a paean to unrequited love – Yorke once admitted that he'd never met a beautiful woman who was also 'nice' – and was brutally to the point, with a chorus that grizzled 'I wish I was special/You're so fucking special/I'm a creep'. Jonny Greenwood, sensing that this latest offering was essentially lightweight, decided to sabotage the tune and unleashed a cataclysmic burst of howling, spine-tingling feedback-drenched guitar, that instead of ruining the effect, enhanced the despairing tone of the song to perfection.

However, when the cut was released as a single in September 1992, it was rejected by all-powerful Radio 1 as being 'too depressing' and faded from view at Number 78 in the UK charts. But that wasn't to be the end of the story – 'Creep' was destined to be one of the great Rip Van Winkles of rock'n'roll. It made the Top 10 in *NME* 's Singles of 1992, while on its back *Melody Maker* picked out the group as the one to watch in 1993. It was also one of the highlights of Radiohead's debut LP which peaked at Number 25 in March 1993.

The song also began to pick up airplay around the world, in the Middle East – notably Israel where it became a Top 30 hit – and then in countries as far-flung as Finland and Australia. Moreover, MTV put the 'Creep' video (shot at the Venue club in the band's hometown) on heavy rotation: one of Thom's abiding memories of his first tour in May 1993 was waking up in a hotel room in Boston at seven in the morning, switching on MTV and seeing the 'Creep' video being broadcast!

The single rocketed up to Number 34 on the Hot 100, rubbing shoulders with other loser anthems like Nirvana's 'Smell Like Teen Spirit'. Such was its success in the land of the brave and the free that it was widely rumoured that the Terminator himself, Arnold Schwarzenegger, wanted to feature the song on the soundtrack to his next movie! The universal acclaim prompted Parlophone to reissue it in the UK, something the band were initially reluctant to do, as bassist Colin Greenwood observed at the time, 'We did all originally agree not to re-release "Creep", but after doing so well in America, there was tremendous pressure from radio people, the press, even our fans to put it out.' 'Creep's second appearance exceeded all expectations and it crashed the Number 7 spot in the UK in September 1993.

However, there was a downside to success. With Parlophone's parent company EMI baying for a follow-up hit single, sessions for the band's second album faltered – the pressures on Yorke were enormous – and eventually plans to record a new single had to be scrapped. For a moment it looked as if the song's notoriety would kill the band, but their tenacity won through and the John Leckie-produced second album, 'The Bends', re-established Radiohead's credentials – even if US record-label personnel initially despaired that the album contained nothing remotely marketable like 'Creep'. Now regarded as one of the great rock anthems of the decade, 'Creep' has gone on to be covered by acts as diverse as Mark Owen, the Pretenders and Tears For Fears!

First released:	1993
Highest UK chart position:	7
Highest US chart position:	34

S ince they first started making music in their native Athens, Georgia, in 1980, REM had spent the best part of a decade garnering the reputation of the biggest cult band in rock. Their songs had many meanings to many people, largely one suspects because of vocalist/lyricist Michael Stipe's unwillingness to enunciate them clearly, but it didn't seem to matter with the guitar-rock of Pete Buck, Mike Mills and Bill Berry offering the same appeal as the Byrds, Tom Petty and generations of bands before.

But REM evolved – they were forced to. Transferring from the independent IRS label to mighty Warner Brothers in a reported $6 million deal raised the stakes and, having made the decision to take the big bucks, a commercial breakthrough was more or less obligatory. While 1989's 'Green' laid the foundations by breaching the US Top 20, the exhausting tour that promoted it nearly broke up the band, and when its successor 'Out Of Time' emerged in 1991 it was to stand or fall on its own merits – no live shows to follow. Much rested on the first single, 'Losing My Religion', and with Stipe singing clearer than he ever had it was ironic that so many different meanings should have been ascribed to his words.

losing my religion

rem

The Times called it 'the first existential pop song ever to make the American Top 10'. It was chosen to preview the album, according to singer Stipe, because 'there's an REM tradition to choose the least likely track as the first single, just to widen the boundaries a bit.' And like so many songs before it, 'Losing My Religion' was musically catchy and lyrically baffling. The fact that Stipe was emoting something so obviously important over a jolly mandolin backing from Buck was surprising enough, but that wasn't the half of it when you came to the words: that's him in the corner, that's him in the spotlight, he's said too much, hasn't said enough… just what is one expected to make of this mass of contradictions?

The title was a Southern saying Stipe had encountered all his life and that he had assumed was in common use elsewhere. 'It's the same as being at the end of your rope, or reaching the final straw and snapping. People have asked me over and over again are you a Catholic, are you a Quaker but this has nothing to do with religion in this song.

'It's used casually – a waitress will say "I almost lost my religion over that table, they were such jerks." To make it more serious, it would be an event so dramatic that it could cause you to question your spiritual beliefs.'

The rock rumour mill would indeed suggest such a dramatic event, insisting that Stipe, a determinedly asexual pop star in image terms, had been diagnosed HIV positive in the six-year interval between tours. 'It bummed me out for ten minutes,' he shrugged of the false rumour, concluding that 'you cannot allow yourself to let the media direct your life.'

Despite this down-to-earth reaction, religion had played a big part in Michael Stipe's upbringing. His grandfather, in his late eighties, had been a travelling preacher for most of his long life, Michael crediting him with passing on 'the performing urge'. He had attended gospel meetings as a child, being brought up in a part of America where 'religion is so ingrained in life… idealized and romanticized, of course, but wildly exciting.' Even so, Stipe always felt 'an outside observer'.

The lyricist had set himself a challenge with 'Out Of Time': it was to be a collection of love songs, with straightforward meanings and less of the ambiguity that had made REM's earlier albums all things to all men. 'Losing My Religion', then, was both a failure and a success. But then this was a man to whom typing errors were a part of his songwriting technique.

For Stipe, the release of 'Losing My Religion' was 'the moment I went from being recognizable to a relatively small, predominantly white audience of 20- to 35-year-olds to having everyone, from black men to young Hispanic kids, checking me as the guy who sang that funny song.' The song in question reached Number 4 in the US chart, while the album it so ably trailed was a transatlantic chart-topper. REM had arrived – and there were many believers.

First released:	1991
Highest UK chart position:	19
Highest US chart position:	4

Noel Gallagher can come up with a good tune – even if someone else has written it first. After years of dance music and rap dominating the charts, Oasis and other Brit-poppers have put strong melodies back in fashion. Noel Gallagher is praised for writing Oasis' hit songs and nearly everything else they've recorded, but echoes of 1960s hits are definitely, maybe, recognized in his work. It begs the question: just how original *is* Noel Gallagher?

With a Burt Bacharach album shown on the cover of their first CD, Oasis wear their influences on their sleeves. Noel Gallagher talks more about the Beatles than Bill Harry and Mark Lewisohn combined. On the cover of 'Live Forever', he put a picture of John Lennon's Liverpool home.

The guitar riff on their first single, 'Supersonic', owed something to George Harrison's 'My Sweet Lord', which in turn – well, you know the story. The second one, 'Shakermaker', wasn't a million miles from the New Seekers' 'I'd Like To Teach The World To Sing'. 'Hello' is an amalgam of Slade's 'Far Far Away' and Gary Glitter's 'Hello Hello I'm Back Again'. 'Don't Look Back In Anger' has shades of Honeybus' 'I Can't Let Maggie Go' and the Casuals' 'Jesamine', not to mention a homage to John Osborne's best-known play. 'Step Out' had its release delayed so that an arrangement could be reached with the publishers of Stevie Wonder's 'Uptight'.

When Oasis recorded 'I Am The Walrus', they did credit Lennon and McCartney as the composers, but Noel must have been tempted. And, irony of ironies, an out-of-court settlement was reached with Neil Innes of the Rutles over the use of 'How Sweet To Be An Idiot'. Oasis draw so heavily on their sources that they are as much a tribute band as No Way Sis. Oasis even sacked their drummer…

For all that, Noel Gallagher can be a fine, original writer, as is shown by Oasis' 1995 Number 2, 'Wonderwall'. The title is suspicious – George Harrison recorded an album of instrumental music called 'Wonderwall' – but no matter, this fine ballad has some great hooks ('You're gonna be the one to save me'), altogether stronger than 'Live Forever'. The lyrics are not as memorable as John and Paul's, but they scan and fit the melody. 'Wonderwall' was a love song for Noel's girlfriend, Meg Matthews, who is pictured on the sleeve of the CD single.

wonderwall

oasis

For all the plagiarism, Noel Gallagher is laddish about his abilities as a songwriter. 'If we were to take anybody's first two albums against my first two albums, I'm there. I'm with the Beatles,' he says confidently. Maybe he is a champagne supernova, but everybody else was covering John and Paul's tunes. The only successful cover of an Oasis tune is 'Wonderwall', recorded by a cabaret singer from a Liverpool seminary calling himself Mike Flowers.

The Mike Flowers Pops pretended that their easy-listening version of 'Wonderwall' had been recorded in the 1960s and the CD contained surface noise. Their version was an excellent joke and made Number 2 in its own right. There is talk of the Three Tenors recording it as well, but does Pavarotti have Liam's charisma? Maybe it will establish Noel Gallagher as the greatest songwriter since, if not Schubert, then Lennon and McCartney.

First released:	1995
Highest UK chart position:	2
Highest US chart position:	8

signs of the times

summertime blues

eddie cochran

I n April 1960, Eddie Cochran was killed in a car crash in Chippenham, Wiltshire. It was the end of a gruelling British tour with Gene Vincent and, coming from California, he hated the English weather. He was about to return to the States with his girlfriend, songwriter Sharon Sheeley, possibly to get married. At 21, he was a year younger than Buddy Holly and, like Holly, he left a considerable legacy of recorded work.

Eddie preferred making records to touring and, back in Hollywood, he was endlessly experimenting with songs, guitar-playing and record production. He is best known for the teenage anthem 'Summertime Blues', the ultimate invitation to party 'C'mon Everybody' and the prophetic 'Three Steps To Heaven'. Chuck Berry was the first rock'n'roller to chronicle the lives of white American teenagers, but he was black and over 30. Eddie Cochran was white and only 18. He could sing in the first person, identify with their hang-ups and appreciate how minor issues could become traumatic events.

The teenager in 'Summertime Blues' is having trouble with his girlfriend, his boss and his parents. Even the Congressman responds, 'I'd like to help you, son, but you're too young to vote' in a stunning, one-line commentary on political life. Eddie is articulating the problem; he doesn't have the solution – 'There ain't no cure for the Summertime Blues.' And he doesn't advocate any drastic action like leaving home. Teenagers were still docile, and when he writes about ' Teenage Heaven', all he wants is a room with a private phone.

Eddie Cochran had the makings of a great producer, as he realized that a record was more than an artist performing a song. Because it has been thought through, 'Summertime Blues' may lack spontaneity. The pauses may be too contrived, but that is hardly a criticism. The defiance of the lyrics in 'Summertime Blues' is matched by the strummed chords of Eddie's guitar. It is so simple and so distinctive. He also overdubbed a guitar part on to the record, which again was unusual for its day. His guitar instrumentals are largely unknown – indeed, some have only recently been released – but they display his preoccupation with obtaining the right sound.

Eddie's songs of teenage angst have proved durable. The Who recorded 'Summertime Blues' live at Leeds – and would Pete Townshend have created 'My Generation' if it wasn't for that song? The song was also an acid-rock hit in the US for Blue Cheer, and Eddie Cochran can also be seen as the father of punk. The Sex Pistols went to Number 3 with both 'C'mon Everybody' and 'Somethin' Else'. They liked the anger and aggression in his songs, but the good-natured humour was probably lost on them.

As Cochran was as good-looking as Presley and living in Hollywood, he would undoubtedly have been offered film roles had he survived. His two-minute cameo performing 'Twenty Flight Rock' in *The Girl Can't Help It* is the highlight of that movie, perhaps of all rock'n'roll movies. When Eddie was asked by Brian Matthew on BBC's *Saturday Club* about his ambitions, he said, 'I want to be successful.' Not a good rock'n'roller, you understand, nor some backroom producer. This man wanted public acclaim and, although rock'n'rollers may deny it, many recordings indicate that he would have become an all-round entertainer. Still, he is remembered as a rock'n'roll legend, and it is not only Heinz who wants to play just like Eddie.

First released:	1958
Highest UK chart position:	18
Highest US chart position:	8

signs of the times

Bob Dylan's first album, released in 1962, was a collection of folk songs, but two original titles gave an indication of what was to come. The album didn't sell, critics couldn't stand his voice and he was regarded by Columbia Records as 'Hammond's folly'. His producer, John Hammond, was given a second chance, and in 1963 'The Freewheelin' Bob Dylan' was released. It contained 13 songs, mostly written by Bob with a little help from old folk tunes. The melody of 'Blowin' In The Wind' itself is derived from the black spiritual 'No More Auction Block For Me'. Dylan's auction block is even available on the bootleg CD, 'Gaslight Tapes'. 'The Freewheelin' Bob Dylan' contained five songs that have become standards of one sort or another – 'Girl From The North Country' (a variant of 'Scarborough Fair'), 'A Hard Rain's A-Gonna Fall', 'Masters Of War', 'Don't Think Twice, It's Alright' and 'Blowin' In The Wind' itself.

blowin' in the wind

bob dylan

In the sleeve notes, Dylan says of 'Blowin' In The Wind', 'I still say that some of the biggest criminals are those that turn their heads away when they see wrong and know it's wrong. I'm only 21 years old and I know that there's been too many wars. You people over 21 should know better.'

The Cold War between Russia and America was at its height and World War 3 was a possibility – even though, with nuclear weapons, the world could be annihilated. The Cuban missile crisis of October 1962 had made Americans wary and Dylan responded with 'A Hard Rain's A-Gonna Fall'. Despite modern warfare, Dylan refers to cannonballs in 'Blowin' In The Wind'. Why does he use such antiquated imagery? The answer, my friend, is that it gives a feeling of history, a theme he developed in 'With God On Our Side' on his next LP, 'The Times They Are A-Changin''.

'Blowin' In The Wind' asks nine questions about peace, including one about civil rights. 'How many years can some people exist before they're allowed to be free?' This led to the song becoming the anthem of the civil rights movement in America. John Lennon envied Dylan's ability to write meaningful songs that enormous crowds could sing – and finally came up with 'Give Peace A Chance'.

Oddly enough, Dylan was not the first person to

perform 'Blowin' In The Wind'. He had written it one day in a coffee house in Greenwich Village. It impressed another performer, Gil Turner, so much that he included the song in his set that night. It was popular in the Village long before Dylan recorded it.

Dylan performs the song sadly and starkly to his own guitar and harmonica accompaniment. His manager, Albert Grossman, had put together a folk trio, Peter, Paul and Mary, as a rival to the Kingston Trio: a group who would take folk songs and sweeten them for public consumption. Peter, Paul and Mary had a hotline to Dylan's work and their version of 'Blowin' In The Wind' climbed to Number 2 on the US charts. In 1966 Stevie Wonder teamed up with Levi Stubbs of the Four Tops for a soul treatment and reprised his arrangement in 1992 for Bob Dylan's 30th Anniversary Concert Celebration. The most poignant interpretation comes from Marlene Dietrich: she recorded the song in German and English.

'Blowin' In The Wind' became the template for protest (or 'finger-pointin'', to use Dylan's description) singers and hundreds of performers followed Bob Dylan's lead. Ironically, not Dylan himself. By 1964, he had had enough and concentrated on writing about personal relationships. One thing is certain: he was no longer Hammond's folly.

First released:	1963
Highest UK chart position:	–
Highest US chart position:	–

signs of the times

At the time of his death, Sam Cooke was firmly established as the leading soul star of the age. Had he lived, there is little doubt he would have cemented his mantle and perhaps gone on to emulate the success of Marvin Gaye, Lionel Richie, Stevie Wonder or James Brown. In short, Sam Cooke possessed the ability to live up to champion boxer Sonny Liston's boast – 'Sam Cooke is the world's greatest rock'n'roll singer, the greatest singer in the world.'

At a time when recording contracts for black singers favoured the record companies, Sam Cooke broke the mould. In 1959 RCA, aware that his contract with Keen was about to expire, offered him a guarantee of $100,000 – a phenomenal sum for a singer at the time, irrespective of his colour. Cooke duly inked with RCA in January the following year and maintained his progress, scoring a million-seller with 'Chain Gang' before the year was out.

Sam Cooke has since entered folklore because of his vocal style, but it is sometimes forgotten just how accomplished a songwriter he was; his 'Cupid' would later provide the likes of Johnny Nash, the Detroit Spinners and Tony Orlando and Dawn with chart success, while Rod Stewart and Otis Redding covered 'Shake'.

He got the inspiration for 'A Change Is Gonna Come' after hearing Bob Dylan's 'Blowin' In The Wind' for the first time. With civil rights very much on the agenda in the US during the mid-1960s, Cooke's song was a timely reminder of the struggle facing the vast majority of the country's black population. Sam's popularity, built on a foundation of gospel-styled songs, was such that the single was a US Top 40 success, but its appeal has transcended the charts and years since.

Sadly, Sam Cooke did not live to see the change he advocated come about, for in December 1964 he was shot

a change is gonna come
sam cooke

to death in a Los Angeles motel. Confusion and contradiction has surrounded the events of that particular night ever since, with the coroner returning a verdict of justifiable homicide against motel manager Bertha Franklin. It was claimed that Cooke had tried to rape a young woman he had checked into the motel with and later attacked the manageress, but despite the claims his popularity with his fans did not diminish in the aftermath: over 200,000 of them are believed to have filed past his coffin paying their respects, a figure that turned his funeral into a chaotic farce.

Although he too was to die young, Otis Redding would prove Cooke's spiritual successor. Producer Jerry Wexler was one of many who recognized this. 'By 1965, when he recorded the album "Otis Blue" after the tragic death of the great Sam Cooke, Redding had become a master. When he sang Sam's "A Change Is Gonna Come", it was clear that the torch had been passed; the tradition was alive.'

First released:	1965
Highest UK chart position:	–
Highest US chart position:	31

eve of destruction

barry mcguire

There are two schools of thought on 'Eve Of Destruction'. Certainly, it is a key protest song, but was it great songwriting or songwriting to a formula? It was written by Phil (P.F.) Sloan, who was known for writing and performing surf songs. Did he genuinely feel that way? And what about the rough-voiced singer, Barry McGuire? He'd been a part of the smooth-singing folk chorale, the New Christy Minstrels. Was he also faking it?

McGuire had been in the Minstrels for four years and was frustrated with the rigidity and repetition of their work. Record producer Lou Adler signed him as a solo artist to the new Dunhill label. Around the same time, Adler had passed a Bob Dylan album to 19-year-old songwriter Phil Sloan and asked him to write something other than surf songs. That night Sloan wrote four protest songs including 'Eve Of Destruction', and his days of writing for Jan and Dean were over.

The backing track for 'Eve Of Destruction' was recorded and McGuire was asked to add his vocal. He says, 'I did "Eve Of Destruction" in one take. Another band was waiting to use the studio so I said I'd come back the following week and do it again. It had mistakes and was out of time but it also had guts and determination.'

Dunhill's vice-president passed the rough cut to a California radio station. The switchboard was jammed by callers wanting to know more about it, so the imperfect take was released. 'I've had people come up to me and say, "Man, that passage where you sing, 'Aaah, you can't twist the truth' is incredible phrasing." No way. I was reading the words and I'd lost my place.'

'Eve Of Destruction' has the world on the brink of nuclear war. 'I don't think it was a protest song,' says McGuire. 'It was more a recognition of truth. When a doctor tells someone he has cancer, he's making a diagnosis, not a protest. Same with "Eve Of Destruction". The song was saying there is a terminal case of greed and moral decay and we're all going to die because of it.'

Although the record was banned by many radio stations, including the BBC, it stormed up the charts on both sides of the Atlantic. It generated a dumb parody by the Spokesmen: 'So over and over again you keep saying it is the end / But I say you're wrong, we're just on the Dawn of Correction.' Despite recording further protest songs, neither McGuire nor Sloan repeated their success. In the aftermath of the Charles Manson atrocities, Barry McGuire dedicated his life to God. He became an ordained minister. He makes Christian records and still tours. He says, 'I often follow "Eve Of Destruction" by "Don't Blame God (For The Sins Of America)" to show that the cause of our problems is man's drive for materialism.'

Phil Sloan got beaten by the system. He didn't have the resilience to sustain a career as a songwriter and Jimmy Webb recorded a fine testimony to him, called simply 'P.F. Sloan'. If Jimmy Webb thinks 'Eve Of Destruction' is a good song, then that's good enough for most people.

Just like a man carrying a placard saying 'The end of the world is nigh', the prophecies in 'Eve Of Destruction' have not taken place. 'That's just where you're wrong,' says Barry McGuire. 'We're still here but a lot of people aren't. There's no reason why all those people in Cambodia and Africa should have died. The song says we're on the eve of destruction and that is the way we're heading. It may take 50 years but that's the way we're going.'

First released:	1965
Highest UK chart position:	3
Highest US chart position:	1

signs of the times

The Beatles, the Rolling Stones and the Animals had solid, timekeeping drummers, but the Who had Keith Moon, a madman playing his oversize kit like a man possessed. Moonie gave the Who their aggression, and his playing encouraged Roger Daltrey to hurl microphones around and Pete Townshend to smash his guitars into speakers. John Entwistle stayed cool, playing a rock-steady bass.

The Who, originally called the High Numbers, were the band for London mods, who were fashion-conscious, scooter-riding teenagers. The Union-Jacketed Who had Top 20 hits with 'I Can't Explain' and 'Anyway Anyhow Anywhere', and while the Beatles were having their rough edges smoothed by Brian Epstein, Kit Lambert and Chris Stamp were encouraging the Who to be as outlandish, and hence as controversial, as possible. Sometimes it got out of hand. Pete Townshend foolishly snapped to the *New Musical Express* that he was performing for 'stupid screaming little girls, morons and idiots'. No one was exempt from the Who's anger.

Townshend, the songwriter of the group, had been impressed by Bob Dylan's first album and one track in particular, 'Talkin' New York'. He fancied writing a talking blues himself, and although it never emerged as a folk song he did keep one phrase, 'Talkin' 'bout my generation'.

In October 1965 Pete took 'My Generation' to a session in London for producer Shel Talmy. He passed the words over to Roger Daltrey. When Roger read them out, he stumbled over Pete's handwriting and stuttered. Manager Kit Lambert said, 'Leave it in.'

who my generation

The music was as fast and as furious as the lyrics were angry, although the live versions with their orgies of instrument-smashing are even more frenzied. 'My Generation' sounded like a hit single and Townshend, a former art student, said, 'Our next single is really Pop Art. It's anti-middle age, anti-boss class, and anti-young marrieds. The big social revolution is that youth, and not age, has become important.' Whatever that might mean. Asked about the wish to die before he got old, he later said, 'We didn't care about ourselves or our future. We wanted to die in plane crashes or get torn to pieces by screaming girls.' This was punk before its time – but not even the Sex Pistols were as negative as this.

The Who argued among themselves and Roger Daltrey was sacked just before 'My Generation' was released. Once it entered the charts, he asked to return. The single climbed to Number 2 and was only kept from the top by the Seekers with 'The Carnival Is Over'. In America, 'My Generation' s-s-s-stuttered its way to Number 74 and the Who didn't attain a Top 20 hit until 'Pinball Wizard' in 1969. The single led to a hard-hitting LP, also called 'My Generation', and encouraged Townshend to become a prolific writer, leading to the rock operas 'Tommy' and 'Quadrophenia': both are also comments on youth culture, albeit from an older perspective.

Not everyone heeded the Who's call to die before they got old. Paul McCartney relished domesticity and sang happily of being a pensioner on 'When I'm 64'. Sadly, the hard-living, hard-drinking Keith Moon f-f-f-faded away after a show-business party in 1978, but the other three members were still around in the mid-1990s, recreating 'Quadrophenia'. Pete Townshend says: 'I've had to live with those words. Every day somebody says, "You hoped you'd die before you got old. What now?"' No doubt, he replies, 'Why don't you all f-f-f-fade away?'

First released:	1965
Highest UK chart position:	2
Highest US chart position:	74

signs of the times

Ground control to Davie Jones. Before 'Space Oddity', David Bowie had released nine singles and an album under the names of Davie Jones, David Bowie and the Manish Boys. Somewhat surprisingly, his biggest inspiration was actor Anthony Newley and the best-known track is the children's novelty single, 'The Laughing Gnome'. Both his songwriting and performing style took a quantum leap with 'Space Oddity'.

The title suggests its origin. David had been to see Stanley Kubrick's film *2001 – A Space Odyssey* which, in 1968, was the ultimate turn-on. The film told of an astronaut lost in space, so David wrote a song about one who had left his 'tin can' thousands of miles above the earth and refused to return. He was so disillusioned by what he saw that he felt better off up there: 'Planet earth is blue and there's nothing I can do'.

space oddity

david bowie

At the time, Rolf Harris was advertising a cheap, pocket instrument called a Stylophone. Marc Bolan was so impressed with this portable keyboard that he gave David one as a present. 'Space Oddity' is probably the only hit to have been written on this example of 'space-age technology', excluding Rolf Harris' own of course. The Anthony Newley influence had gone, and this time the melody had a similar feel to the Bee Gees' 'New York Mining Disaster'.

David was to make a new album with producer Tony Visconti, but Visconti decided that 'Space Oddity' was too commercial and recommended Gus Dudgeon. Dudgeon was later to produce another space classic, Elton John's 'Rocket Man'. He asked Paul Buckmaster to arrange the strings and the musicians were guitarist Mick Wayne, bassist Herbie Flowers, drummer Terry Cox (Pentangle), and Rick Wakeman on mellotron. Each musician was given £9 for their efforts.

The Moonshot was in the news and Bowie's manager, Ken Pitt, used it to extract as much publicity as possible. He arranged for the song to be played at the Rolling Stones concert in Hyde Park and his efforts paid off, as the single climbed to Number 5. It did not meet with similar success in America as listeners, charged with Neil Armstrong's achievement, did not want negative songs about astronauts. The song was later reissued to greater success and it only became a UK Number 1 in 1975. It was the first time a reissue had made the top.

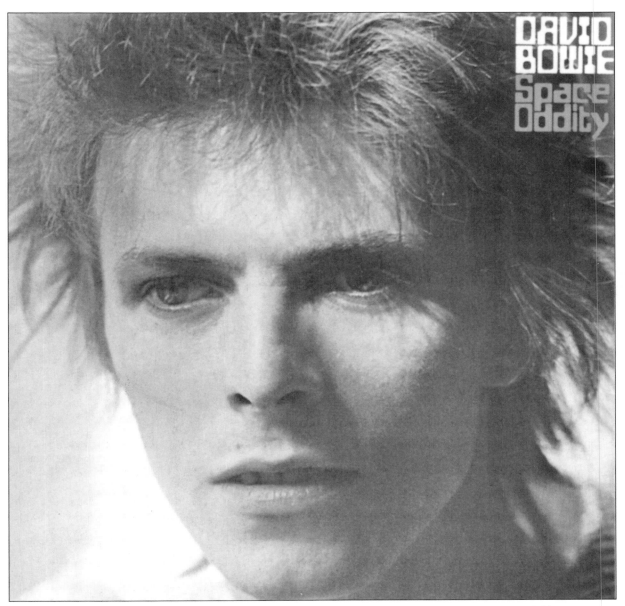

DAVID BOWIE Space Oddity

It has been suggested that 'Space Oddity' is about heroin addiction, with the dealer (ground control) giving instructions to the junkie (Major Tom). It's possible, because David did experiment with heroin in 1968. Also, in 1980 Bowie produced his chart-topping follow-up to 'Space Oddity', 'Ashes To Ashes'. Major Tom was no longer floating in a most peculiar way. He'd become the man who fell to earth and as he sings, 'Ashes to ashes, funk to funky/We know Major Tom's a junkie.' There is also a stunning acoustic version of 'Space Oddity' with just Mick Ronson on bass.

The Barron Knights wanted to parody 'Space Oddity', making it a story of two cats – Major Tom, of course. Bowie's publishers refused permission, but the group met Bowie on *Top Of The Pops*, who said yes. Maybe the Thin White Duke isn't a weirdo after all.

First released:	1969
Highest UK chart position:	1
Highest US chart position:	15

woodstock
matthews' southern comfort

Despite being the queen of confessional songwriting, Joni Mitchell has written few hit songs, but then she has never been interested in the 'starmaker machinery'. Her only UK hit has been with the ecological novelty song 'Big Yellow Taxi', and her only US Top 20 hit with a touching love song, 'Help Me'. Her songs have been sung by others, notably 'This Flight Tonight' (Nazareth), 'Both Sides Now' (Judy Collins) and 'Woodstock' (Matthews' Southern Comfort).

The Woodstock festival took place in August 1969 at Max Yasgur's farm in New York State. It featured Jimi Hendrix, the Who, Joe Cocker, Santana and Crosby, Stills and Nash, but not Bob Dylan, who was recuperating from a motorcycle accident nearly in Woodstock itself. David Crosby had produced Mitchell's first album and she was living with Graham Nash, so CSN asked Joni to join them on stage. Because of her other commitments, she was travelling on her own by car, but so many hippies were going to the festival ('half a million strong') that the roads were blocked. She gave up and returned to a hotel room in New York. There, watching the event on TV, she wrote 'Woodstock'. It encapsulated the festival's feelings of love and peace.

Joni put her hymn-like 'Woodstock' on to 'Ladies Of The Canyon', an impressive album which also included 'Big Yellow Taxi' and 'The Circle Game'. In the UK, Ian Matthews had left Fairport Convention in 1969 and formed a new band with an American name, Matthews' Southern Comfort. Ian remembers, 'I bought Joni's album and we had to do four songs on a BBC lunchtime show. We only had three rehearsed but I liked "Woodstock". I worked up an arrangement and we did it live. We got such a strong response that we put it out as a single. Crosby, Stills and Nash did it too but the only comparison is that it's the same song. Their treatment is totally different to ours. We're very laid back.'

Because Crosby, Stills and Nash belonged to the same group of record labels in the States, Matthews' Southern Comfort's version of 'Woodstock' could not be released until CSN had had a stab at the charts. They went to Number 11 and then Matthews' Southern Comfort made the Top 40. In the UK, Matthews' Southern Comfort were luckier, with the single staying at Number 1 for three weeks until it was replaced by the star of Woodstock, Jimi Hendrix. Matthews' Southern Comfort did not have further hits because Ian disbanded it to concentrate on his own, somewhat eclectic career. He is a highly regarded performer, who lives in America but often performs in the United Kingdom.

Although Joni Mitchell did not appear at Woodstock, she did make the Isle of Wight festival, where she had to cope with interruptions from the Maoists who wanted to make it a free festival. She used considerable personal courage to quieten them and the huge crowd was wholly on her side as she sang 'Woodstock'.

First released:	1970
Highest UK chart position:	1
Highest US chart position:	23

Four major talents came together when Neil Young joined the already successful superstar trio of Crosby, Stills and Nash in 1969. With four singer-songwriters aboard, the competition was such that Young made only two contributions to their Top 5 album 'Déjà Vu', which consequently overflowed with peace-and-love vibes as epitomized by Graham Nash's sentimental 'Our House'. The most famous single track from it was 'Woodstock', written by Nash's then girlfriend Joni Mitchell to celebrate the rock festival of that name. But this, and 'Déjà Vu's overwhelming optimism, was very much at odds with Vietnam and the Draft as the peace-and-love 1960s turned into the cynical 1970s.

Neil Young sensed the mood, and it was his reaction to events at Kent State University that would be the band's next release. On 4 May 1970, US National Guardsmen killed four students protesting against the conflict in south-east Asia. A shocked Young was inspired to respond in song, and the result was 'Ohio', which was rush-released as a single just days later.

Young and Crosby had been staying with their road manager in Pecadero, a small coastal village 30 miles south of San Francisco, as news of the tragedy broke. A heated discussion ended with Young withdrawing from proceedings and picking up his guitar. 'Ohio', its stinging denouncement topped by the plaintive, angry chorus 'Four dead in Ohio', would itself draw fire from high places when vice-president Spiro Agnew denounced it –

and rock music generally – as being 'anti-US'. But then this was an era when people believed music *could* change the world…

Crosby and Young summoned Nash and Stills, who had flown in from England, to the Record Plant studio in Los Angeles, where they met bassist Fuzzy Samuels and drummer John Barbata. The session moved Crosby to tears, as the end result did many listeners. Young himself nominated 'Ohio' as his best ever CSN&Y cut in his liner notes to 'Decade' in 1977, adding: 'It's still hard to believe I had to write this song. It's still ironic that I capitalized on the death of these American students. Probably the biggest lesson learned at an American place of learning.'

David Crosby saw the song as much more than just cheap sloganeering. 'I don't think musicians should go and seek stands out,' he blustered, 'but when something slaps you in the face personally you have to respond to it… Even Neil couldn't stand it. He had to respond… it was as genuine and honest a thing as you could ask for.'

The single beat an airplay ban to rise to Number 14 in the US chart, backed with chilling appropriateness (and in echoes of Buffalo Springfield's quasi-democratic writing policy) with a live version of Steve Stills' 'Find The Cost Of Freedom'. Stills' own political awareness had surfaced in Buffalo Springfield some three years earlier with 'For What It's Worth', a song he had been inspired to write by police oppression on Sunset Strip.

Young would leave Crosby, Stills and Nash to resume his own solo career with no little success, although

ohio

crosby, stills, nash and young

another version of 'Ohio' would emerge on 1971's 'Four Way Street', a live souvenir of the short-lived supergroup that hit US Number 1 status. An even more impassioned live take appeared on the following year's *Journey Through The Past* soundtrack, one of Young's less commercial efforts.

Young would not rejoin his colleagues until 1988, when 'American Dream' saw him once again adding an acid edge to his saccharine cohorts. 'Ohio' was now two decades away and no longer on the agenda, but you sensed that Young at least had not forgotten.

First released:	1970
Highest UK chart position:	–
Highest US chart position:	14

A song can still be a great song even if no one's heard it, hence the inclusion of John Stewart's account of the moon landing, 'Armstrong'. Stewart had come to prominence in the Kingston Trio and left to become a solo performer. His 1969 album, 'California Bloodlines', made across the street from Bob Dylan's 'Nashville Skyline', included his song about love on the road, 'July, You're A Woman'. ('Elvis liked that song and used to sing it in his dressing-room. He never recorded it but with all these sightings, I haven't given up hope.'). In 1979, after making several albums of his own material, he won a gold disc with a song about wanting a hit record, 'Gold', but he failed to make a lasting impression. He wrote 'Runaway Train', which was a US country hit for Rosanne Cash. Luckily, the royalties from the Monkees' 'Daydream Believer' kept him afloat.

armstrong

john stewart

And so to 'Armstrong'. In 1969, Neil Armstrong, the commander of the US spacecraft Apollo 11, became the first man to set foot on the moon. Televised pictures were sent back to earth, and who can forget his first words: 'One small step for man, one giant leap for mankind'? (Thirty years on this sounds suspiciously like a soundbite coined by marketing people, but we were more gullible then.)

John Stewart wrote the song as the event was unfolding. He went into the studios on 25 July and the single he recorded incorporated a snatch of Neil Armstrong's voice. The single was released in the US by Capitol on 18 August, which shows that record companies can pull their fingers out when they want to. It was a powerful, evocative song, all the more so for Stewart's vibrato. Stewart says, 'The message of the song was that even though there are ghettos in Chicago and people are starving in India and we've completely ravaged the planet, we could for one moment sit there and watch one of our kind walk on the moon. Where we have really failed we have also succeeded greatly.'

Then everything went wrong. 'Everyone took it as a putdown of the Moonshot, which was not intended at all,' says Stewart now. 'It was banned on radio stations and some stations were even breaking the record on the air. It got on the charts at Number 80 and the next week it got to Number 50 and then it disappeared.'

'Armstrong' might well have been a hit in the UK but it was never released here. It did, however, appear in a new version on John's 1973 album, 'Cannons In The Rain'.

The Byrds recorded a song about the three astronauts on Apollo 11, 'Armstrong, Aldrin And Collins', a gentle folk song thanking God which has none of the impact of John Stewart's song. The astronauts brought back samples of moon rock, inspiring a song by Dory Previn which again is fairly nondescript.

These days, Stewart comes to the UK on an annual tour and plays small rooms at the back of pubs. He visits the same cities (York, Edinburgh) and the shows are like gatherings of friends. He makes his own tapes and singles for sale, and in 1994 he had a CD single of a new version of 'Armstrong' together with a six-minute narrative, 'The Witness', giving his further thoughts on that July afternoon. Nothing, however, can be more compelling than the final lines of his song:

'And I wonder if a long time ago somewhere in the universe,

They watched a man named Adam walk upon the earth.'

First released:	1970
Highest UK chart position:	—
Highest US chart position:	50

Ostensibly John Lennon's finest song, the origins of 'Imagine' are in fact with Yoko Ono. She published a book of poems in 1970 called *Grapefruit*, which had an introduction by Lennon. 'Imagine' was a recurrent word in her poems, with such instructions as 'Imagine one thousand suns in the sky at the same time'. The word inspired Lennon, and just before his death he told the broadcaster Andy Peebles, '"Imagine" should be credited as a Lennon/Ono song. A lot of it, the lyric and the concept, came from Yoko, but those days I was a bit more selfish, a bit more macho and I omitted to mention her contribution, which was right out of *Grapefruit*. She's just the wife and you don't put her name on it, right?'

What's more, the song was written on Yoko's piano. John had given it to her as a birthday present and the inscription read, 'This morning a white piano for Yoko.' The white piano was in keeping with their love of white rooms and, even now, you never seen Yoko in anything but black or white.

imagine

john lennon

Lennon's first solo album, 'John Lennon/Plastic Ono Band', had been stark and uncompromising, and a bitter song like 'Working Class Hero' with his four-letter words would never get airplay. With songs like 'Imagine', it was clear that this album would be more radio-friendly. The songs were recorded at home – John called it 'the Ascot sound' – and 'Imagine' itself features only John on piano, Klaus Voormann on bass and Alan White on drums.

Producer Phil Spector then took the tracks to New York where he added strings, but this was not one of his overblown Wall of Sound productions. The sympathetic arrangement to 'Imagine' turns the song into a lullaby and John described the album as 'electric twentieth-century folk music'.

Because John was a rudimentary pianist, 'Imagine' has an elementary tune and the piano sounds strangely off-key at the beginning. The lyric was as much spoken as sung and it was performed slowly, quietly and hypnotically. John is inviting listeners to share his dream, although he does not indicate how the Brotherhood of Man might be achieved. John Lennon was echoing Charlie Chaplin's thoughts of being a world citizen without boundaries or differences. The song decries religion, nationalism and capitalism, and yet the Conservative Party used it during the 1987 election.

'Imagine' is not specifically about socialism, although its leanings are obvious. Paul McCartney told *Melody Maker*, '"Imagine" is what John is really like. There was too much political stuff on the other album.' John retorted, 'So you think "Imagine" isn't political? It's "Working Class Hero" with sugar on for conservatives like yourself.'

Not everyone has been impressed by 'Imagine'. Lennon's second assassin, biographer Albert Grossman, called it 'a hippie wishing-well full of pennyweight dreams for a better world. "Imagine" suffers from a piano accompaniment as monotonous as a student in a practice room and a vocal delivery as feeble as a hymn sung in a Quaker parlour.'

The public would never agree. In October 1971 the single entered the US charts and climbed to Number 3. It wasn't released in the UK until 1975 and made Number 6. After John's death, the song took on a new meaning and topped the chart. There are hundreds of versions of 'Imagine' including those by Joan Baez, Randy Crawford, Petula Clark, Elton John and Ben E. King. None can match Lennon's own because, when we hear it, we hear a man with his own personal dream for a better world.

First released:	1971
Highest UK chart position:	1
Highest US chart position:	3

signs of the times

what's goin' on marvin gaye

The tragic death of Tammi Terrell on 16 March 1970 not only deprived the soul music world of a great talent, but also killed off any enthusiasm Marvin Gaye had for the recording industry. So devastated was he by the passing of his most successful singing partner, that he did not tour or perform live for a couple of years. More importantly, he could not be cajoled into returning to the studio either, so only a number of previously recorded and released singles ensured his name remained in the public eye.

Instead, Marvin went into semi-retirement. 'I was terribly disillusioned with a lot of things in life, and in life in general. I decided to take time out to try to do something about it. In a sense the rumours that suggested I had quit were true. I had retired, but only from the personal appearance end.'

About the only things Marvin was interested in at the time were sport (he made a half-hearted attempt to get signed up by the Detroit Lions, an American Football team!) and his family, especially his younger brother Frankie, who was serving in the US Armed Forces in Vietnam. For most families, the horrors of Vietnam were something they saw only on the television screens during the nightly news bulletins, but for Marvin the full nightmare was being recounted first-hand by his brother.

Producer Al Cleveland and Renaldo 'Obie' Benson (of the Four Tops) had written a tune that they felt would sit comfortably with Marvin's vocal delivery, and they left a tape for Marvin to have a listen to. Marvin couldn't be persuaded even to listen to it for two months; he had to hear more from Frankie. Then, at some point, Marvin felt he had to tell people what his brother was going through out in Vietnam: 'It's so weird man, what is happening God, what is happening Lord, what is going on with life and people? I don't know.' So Marvin set about writing lyrics that brought his thoughts about Vietnam to life. Then he heard Al and Obie's tune, and fitted the two together.

Marvin originally planned to give the song to the Originals (he had been responsible for penning their hit 'Baby I'm For Real') but subsequently decided to record it himself. He also couldn't wait for Al Cleveland to return to Detroit, choosing instead to produce himself for the first time. He brought a number of friends into the studio for the recording session, including Bobby Rogers (of the Miracles), Lem Barney and Mel Farrer (of the Detroit Lions!), resulting in an almighty row with Motown, who tried to demand Marvin use professional backing singers. But Marvin held his ground. 'It worked just perfectly. "Hey man, what's happening, hey baby!" Slap thighs, slapped hands. Man, it was great, just what I wanted.'

It wasn't what Motown wanted, however, and neither was the resulting album. Berry Gordy tried to put off releasing either, and only did so to try to prove to Marvin that neither was likely to appeal to the public. In the event, it was Berry who lost the argument: the single sold in excess of 70,000 in its first week, and subsequently topped the R&B charts (for five weeks) and hit Number 2 on the pop listings, with the album peaking at Number 6.

In the UK, the fact that the overall sound was such a radical departure from the accepted Marvin Gaye sound perhaps made it difficult to promote, although Marvin's name alone should have ensured a chart placing of some sort. Instead, both the single and album have since had to enjoy a reputation derived entirely from their importance to black music. Little wonder, then, that Marvin's 'What's Goin' On' has become one of Motown's steadiest-selling catalogue items.

First released:	1971
Highest UK chart position:	–
Highest US chart position:	2

streets of london

ralph mctell

Every major UK city has homeless people selling *The Big Issue* and thousands are sleeping rough. The situation is getting worse, and a simple indicator is listening to Ralph McTell's 'Streets Of London'. The song contains four verses and they are about old men and women carrying their homes 'in two carrier-bags'. At that time it was rare to see someone under fifty on the streets of London. The question could now be asked, where have all the old men gone?

'Streets Of London' can be taken as a companion to 'Waterloo Sunset'. Ray Davies is optimistic as he sees love through the grim landscape: McTell looks at the same streets and sees despair. Ralph wrote it after busking around Europe. It was going to be about the poor people of Paris, but as there was already a song of that title, he switched it to London. He comments: 'I'd only written two songs before "Streets Of London", which had started out in 1965 as an instrumental. One was about the Ku Klux Klan and the other was for my girlfriend, Nanna. I included "Nanna's Song" on the first album but I didn't include "Streets Of London" as I thought it was too down and maybe people wouldn't like it.'

Ralph wasn't even performing the song, but it was taken up by another folksinger, Derek Brimstone. He got a good reaction to it, and when he next saw Ralph he told him how well it was going. Ralph started to perform it himself, but it was only with reluctance that he included it on his second album, 'Spiral Staircase'.

To Ralph's surprise, the song became the most popular one on the album and was soon a standard around UK folk clubs. By 1974 he had moved from the specialist Transatlantic label to the mainstream Reprise, and it was suggested that he re-record 'Streets Of London' with a gentle rock backing, strings and a girl chorus. It upset purists, but McTell couldn't complain as he had produced it himself. Again to his surprise, he found himself singing about homelessness on *Top Of The Pops*. How apt that 'Lonely This Christmas' should be followed by 'Streets Of London' on the Christmas chart, although to keep things in perspective, 'Wombling Merry Christmas' was Number 3.

The song was not a hit in the US, but it has been recorded by many American acts. Also, Kinky Friedman's 'Sold American' has much the same feel as 'Streets Of London'. 'A lot of singers say, "We're going to do a sincere song,"' says McTell, 'and they put too much emotion into it. They don't need to. One of the best versions is by Harry Belafonte and he practically talks the lyrics.'

Ralph McTell appealed to a new generation with the children's TV shows *Alphabet Zoo* and *Tickle On The Tum*, but all the while he was recording albums of thought-provoking, sometimes political, material. The songs are often better crafted than 'Streets Of London' because, let's be honest, 'And say for you that the sun don't shine' is a badly constructed line. No one speaks like that.

McTell is an accomplished guitarist and he also records blues songs. At every concert he performs 'Streets Of London'and maybe he has grown weary of it after 30 years. 'Not at all,' he says. 'As soon as I start to play, I close my eyes and I can see the pictures as if it were yesterday. I can never sing the song without being aware of what I'm singing about, thank God for that.'

First released:	1974
Highest UK chart position:	2
Highest US chart position:	–

If ever rock'n'roll needed a kick up the rear, it was back in 1976 when all inspiration seemed to evaporate in a welter of concept albums, banal country-rock and stadium gigs. Help was at hand and, as winter turned into spring 1977, Britain bristled with an almost supernatural energy as punk rock rang out the old with a vengeance. Spearheading the new movement were the Sex Pistols and the Clash, two very different sides of the same coin. The Pistols revelled in a profound and destructive nihilism, while the Clash shone with both a political and idealistic positivism. The band had formed in 1976 from the ashes of the London SS and the 101ers, and by the time they played the legendary 100 Club Punk Festival that September had settled on a fairly stable line-up of singer Joe Strummer, guitarist Mick Jones, bassist Paul Simonon and drummer Terry Chimes, although the latter, at odds with the rest of the band's political stance, would quit to be replaced by Topper Headon, thus completing the classic line-up which would persist until 1982.

1977

clash

Signing to CBS, and with live sound man Micky Foote in charge giving them a treble-heavy mix, the band set about recording their debut single and album with indecent haste. The result was the release of the 'White Riot' 45 and its parent LP, simply titled 'The Clash', within a week of each other in February 1977. The album was destined for the Number 12 spot and a four-month chart residency, while the single peaked at Number 38.

The music was amphetamined (the preferred drug of the new generation) and furious, with Strummer's leather-tonsilled voice chanting the message-laden lyrics sometimes inaudibly over the top. 'White Riot' was a revelation. Inspired by the clashes between police and mainly black youths at the previous year's Notting Hill Carnival, it was Strummer's cry to arms for the disaffected white kids coming of age at that time. The B-side, '1977', was more prophetic. Over a primeval guitar riff that was cruder than even anything off the Kinks' first album from over a decade previously, and Chimes's brutal staccato drumming, Strummer highlighted his complaints against society and life in general: unemployment; life on the never-never; the rich getting richer. In a staggering 1 minute 40 seconds, this vitriolic diatribe closely echoed the sentiments of the Pistols' 'No Future'.

signs of the times

Perhaps the best-remembered line was 'In 1977, no Elvis, no Beatles, no Rolling Stones' which signalled one of punk's main objectives – to replace the fat old self-satisfied dinosaurs of rock with a new, more vital and relevant brand of music. Ironically, Strummer and Jones, when penning the song, couldn't have foreseen that come August 1977 there would indeed be no Elvis, as the American grand-daddy of rock'n'roll would himself be dead. The song became an anthem for the watershed year of the decade – the punks hijacked the Queen's Silver Jubilee celebrations for their own ends and, with constant clashes between safety-pin festooned youths and the police, 1977 went down as hosting the 'Summer of Hate'.

Furthermore, the Clash were instrumental in bringing black and white closer together and popularizing reggae, which became a huge influence as punk rock gave way to the cooler, more expansive New Wave. Rastafarian band Culture released the similarly titled 'When Two Sevens Clash' at the close of the year, declaring that according to

their religious calendar, not only was social disorder rife but apocalypse was at hand. In the event, it wasn't quite the end of the world, but their single was magnificent.

By 1978 the Clash were experimenting away from their garage-band roots, incorporating many Jamaican influences into their sound and even recording with Blue Oyster Cult producer Sandy Pearlman on the ironically named 'Give Em Enough Rope' LP. However, '1977' remains the embodiment of the prototype savage young Clash, and a typically machine-gun rapid version was a highlight of their posthumous 'Clash On Broadway' three-CD boxed set.

First released:	1977
Highest UK chart position:	–
Highest US chart position:	–

signs of the times

Malcolm McLaren, the Sex Pistols' manager and provocateur, knew the value of publicity. The public, he thought, were tiring of rock superstars like Rod Stewart and Elton John, and hating the posturing of Roxy Music and long set-pieces from Emerson, Lake and Palmer. His group of four disaffected London lads would appeal to certain youth elements and outrage everyone else.

The ploy worked better than even McLaren could have imagined. The group was signed to EMI and a single, 'Anarchy In The UK', was released. Following an ill-tempered, four-lettered television exchange with veteran broadcaster Bill Grundy, supplies of the single were withdrawn and the band was paid £50,000 to leave the label.

A&M then signed the Pistols, but a protest from other stars made them renege on the deal. This time, the Pistols collected £75,000. With some reluctance, the Pistols signed with Richard Branson's Virgin.

god save the queen

sex pistols

John Lydon, who became Johnny Rotten, wrote the lyrics to 'No Future' while living in a Hampstead squat. It was arranged, quite competently as it happens, by the other Pistols – Steve Jones (guitar), Glen Matlock (bass) and Paul Cook (drums). Admittedly, Rotten had a job staying in tune – as if he cared – but this only added to the effect. McLaren saw the song as an alternative national anthem and renamed it after its first line, 'God Save The Queen'. Virgin announced that their first Pistols' single was to be 'God Save The Queen' and hell broke loose. The pressing plant refused to press the single and the printers the sleeve, so these disputes had to be resolved.

In truth, the song's lyrics mean little. To call Britain 'a fascist regime' means that Johnny Rotten hadn't a clue what he was writing about. John Peel played the single twice and then both the BBC and IBA banned it on grounds of bad taste.

The single came out just before the Silver Jubilee of the Queen's accession to the throne. Royalists threatened violence against the Pistols and Jamie Reid, who designed the cover which defaced a picture of Her Majesty, had his leg broken. The Pistols allegedly threatened to kill DJ Bob Harris for not playing their records.

Not only did the public have difficulty hearing the single, they also had trouble buying it. W.H. Smith, Woolworths and Boots refused to stock it. Many people bought it in Virgin's own stores. It came into the chart at Number 10 and looked as though it would be at the top during Jubilee week itself.

Anxious to avoid such a record at Number 1, the authorities came to an instant decision – shops that sold their own records could not be included in the chart. Hence, Virgin's sales were ignored for the purposes of compiling the chart and Rod Stewart stayed at Number 1 with 'I Don't Want To Talk About It'.

After that, the Pistols did another nihilistic single, 'Pretty Vacant', but they soon disbanded, with Rotten being replaced for a one-off release by Great Train Robber Ronnie Biggs. Sid Vicious, who had replaced Glen Matlock before 'God Save The Queen' was released, died

of a drugs overdose while on bail for murdering his girlfriend. The Sex Pistols lasted just over a year as a chart act, but they had opened the door for other confrontational groups.

In 1996 the Sex Pistols re-formed, and Radio 1 broadcast a whole concert live. In 1997 EMI, who now own the Virgin catalogue, issued a special edition of their LP 'Never Mind The Bollocks, Here's The Sex Pistols', to celebrate 100 years of EMI. One track on the LP is the Sex Pistols' bitter thoughts about EMI…

First released:	1977
Highest UK chart position:	2
Highest US chart position:	–

signs of the times

Whether punk music evolved as a reaction to rock and pop or as a progression has remained a constant source of debate in the two decades or so since it first reared its often ugly head; but there is little doubt that punk made a lasting impact on the development of music. Not least was the ability of writers to draw inspiration from a reservoir of ideas previously unexplored: there were no taboos with punk music. In the late summer of 1977, one such record hit the charts – the Adverts' 'Gary Gilmore's Eyes'.

Gilmore was an American killer who had demanded the right to be executed by firing squad, a somewhat strange request since no one had been executed by such means since the Second World War. Once he got his wish and the Adverts their hit single, it was obvious that anything went in the world, and especially pop. While the Adverts were raising eyebrows with their hit, another group closely allied to the growing punk movement were making their first assault on the charts.

The Boomtown Rats had evolved from the Nightlife Thugs and, led by ex-journalist Bob Geldof, had been picking up fans and accolades by the score with a succession of hit singles. 'Rat Trap', a UK Number 1 in 1978, represented something of a departure from their normal fast and frantic punk output, and was an indication of a shift towards more structured and textured songs for the future. In the meantime, the group were preparing a launch on the US market and journeyed to the States for promotional work and live dates.

The events at Hungerford (1987) and Dunblane (1996) have brought home the full horrors of one madman running amok with shotguns and firearms, but in 1979 in Britain such events were still relatively unknown. This was not the case in America, where at times it seemed as though there was at least one madman (or woman) every month shooting his or her way into the history books. On 29 January 1979 it was the turn of schoolgirl Brenda Spencer, who shot and killed several of her classmates. She was subsequently captured and asked why she had

i don't like mondays

boomtown rats

done what she had. 'I don't like Mondays' was her only reply. The comment came to the attention of Geldof, who quickly put together a song that used the phrase as its hook.

While British audiences remained somewhat ignorant of the circumstances surrounding the inspiration for the song, they took to the single, sending it to Number 1 in only two weeks and keeping it there for four. The record met with considerable resistance in the US, where Brenda Spencer's parents tried to have it banned on the grounds that it would prejudice the impending court case involving their daughter. They needn't have bothered, for many radio stations refused to playlist the single on the grounds of taste anyway.

In 1980 the single was rightly honoured at the Ivor Novello Awards ceremony: Best Pop Song and Outstanding British Lyric.

First released:	1979
Highest UK chart position:	1
Highest US chart position:	73

another brick in the wall

pink floyd

For many years, British progressive rock giants Pink Floyd went out of their way not to release singles – and their album sales undoubtedly benefited as a result, as well as giving them a reputation as a 'credible' group keen to distance themselves from the fads and fashions of the singles market. This was despite an initial rash of 1960s success with such whimsical ditties as 'Arnold Layne' and 'See Emily Play'.

By 1980, the singer of those songs, Syd Barrett, was long gone: the man behind this single and the concept album 'The Wall' to which it was in effect the title track was bassist/vocalist Roger Waters, and the project was borne of the gruelling tour-album-tour schedule that had occupied the band for the whole of the 1970s. After 'freaking out' in Montreal and spitting at a fan in the front row, Waters speculated on the nature of the alienation that can build up between performers and their audience – an imaginary wall.

A 160-foot real wall was built across the stage for performances, but the song's success was due to the unusually catchy chorus sung in part by schoolchildren, whose addition was a last-minute idea from guitarist Dave Gilmour. 'I sent the tape to England and got an engineer to summon some kids. I gave him a whole set of instructions – 10- to 15-year-olds from North London, mostly boys – and said get them to sing as many ways as you like.'

Transferred to 24-track tape, the kids were promoted from background vocals to deliver an actual verse, in ironic imitation of concert performances where groups encourage their fans to sing – and it was the implied insolence that led South African apartheid authorities to ban the song when it was used by striking children. Whereas a song like Alice Cooper's 'School's Out' had been rampantly hedonistic, 'Another Brick In The Wall (Part 2)' – to give it its full title, Part 1 being a previous album track – questioned the way schools tame the human spirit. A menacing animated video from Gerald Scarfe, the cartoonist who created the album cover, drove the point home.

'The Wall' spawned a 1982 film starring Boomtown Rat Bob Geldof, while Waters – who left the band amid acrimony three years later – would re-stage the album live at the site of the Berlin Wall in Potzdamer Platz. Featuring Bryan Adams, Van Morrison, Joni Mitchell and others, the event was broadcast live throughout the world, and raised money for the Memorial Fund for Disaster Relief. As composer, he was entitled to 'cover' his own song even if Dave Gilmour, Rick Wright and Nick Mason, his fellow musicians on the recording, were now operating as Pink Floyd without him. His remains the only rival version of the song to have seen release. In chart terms the original was very much a one-off, becoming the band's first and only chart-topper in both the UK and US.

The album was equally successful, topping the *Billboard* chart for 15 weeks and selling over eight million in the US alone. This was just as well, since the collapse of the company that had advised the Floyd on their financial investments had brought them to the brink of financial disaster. 'The Wall' would prove vital in giving the Floyd empire a much-needed new foundation.

First released:	1979
Highest UK chart position:	1
Highest US chart position:	1

As punk gave way to New Wave at the end of the 1970s, various musical scenes as diverse as power pop and mod coexisted happily with each other. But arguably the most important and most successful was the 2 Tone phenomenon, which drew heavily on reggae's precursors, bluebeat and ska, marrying their dance rhythms with New Wave pop sensibility and punk's social conscience.

2 Tone was the brainchild of keyboards player Gerald Dankin, aka Jerry Dammers, who in the *sturm und drang* summer of 1977 formed a reggae/punk-influenced outfit in his native Coventry. Known variously as the Coventry Automatics and the Coventry Specials, the group settled on the name the Special AKA and quickly established a reputation for themselves on account of the heavy ska flavour of their music. Ska and its counterpart bluebeat had once, curiously, been the property of the right-wing skinhead movement, so it was doubly fascinating that this multi-racial group was now claiming it back as their own.

Dammers set up the group's own label, 2 Tone, the name of which would be adopted for the wider movement and play host to similar bands like Madness, the Beat and the Bodysnatchers. It also proved the launchpad for a number of hit albums and singles by the band themselves, who had trimmed down their name to the Specials.

While many took the band at face value and were content to groove to their eminent danceability – the Specials were featured in the *Dance Craze* movie in 1981 – the critics especially latched on to Dammers' often acutely social and political lyrics. Songs like 'Concrete Jungle' and 'Rat Race' swiftly established his credentials as a songwriter who matched the eloquence of a Paul Weller or Elvis Costello.

In 1981 the Specials were at the zenith of their career, and the 'Ghost Town' single was destined to follow up the success of their live EP (which contained the teen anthem 'Too Much Too Young') and give them a second Number 1 for three weeks in July. Although supposedly written about Dammers' hometown, 'Ghost Town' was viewed in a wider social context. It was a prophetic recording. The Conservatives were half-way through their first term in office, and while the 'yuppie' revolution was triumphantly under way, social services and housing were already feeling the blade of the Thatcherite knife. Inner-city riots were becoming commonplace around the country – copycat scenes of looting and pillaging were flashed around the nation's TV networks.

ghost town
specials

Middle-class England looked on in terror as riots in places as far away as Toxteth and Brixton flared up on their screens in the privacy of their own homes. Urban decay was ignored as the Tories preached about law and order, about giving the police force more power and about dealing more deftly with youthful offenders. In contrast, the song was almost low key, with a sparse bass line giving it its centre and the vocals restrained too, especially after the full-blooded, brass-laden workouts of earlier hits like 'A Message To You Rudy'.

The single was in no small way aided by a superb promo video (all shadows and eerily lit in an Orson Welles-type of way), which depicted the band in glorious monotone driving around a deserted cityscape. Its three-week Number 1 run was all the more of an achievement given that this was the year of the ostrich-like New Romantics, whose values were diametrically opposed to those of the 2 Tone movement.

Sadly, 'Ghost Town' marked the end of the Specials – shortly afterwards, Hall, Golding and Staples defected to form the enjoyable but ultimately lightweight Fun Boy Three, and although Dammers reverted to the Special AKA name and kept the ideals afloat for a while longer, his songwriting as evinced on the likes of 'Free Nelson Mandela' (a Top 10 hit in 1984) never quite attained the deft subtlety and poignancy of earlier successes like 'Ghost Town'.

First released:	1981
Highest UK chart position:	1
Highest US chart position:	—

white lines (don't don't do it)

grandmaster flash and melle mel

Of all musical styles and genres, none is perhaps as misunderstood or maligned as rap. Much of the problem rests with the artists and the songs themselves: aggressive names, with songs that are denigrative towards women, the police and authority, contain bad language or advocate the free use of guns are hardly likely to endear themselves to the pop record buyer. It is therefore no surprise that rap music albums and singles were responsible virtually single-handedly for the introduction of 'Parental Guidance' stickers!

For all its faults, rap music has had a number of great moments, and for one reason or another Sugarhill Records has been responsible for most of them. It was Sugarhill that first made rap popular. And it was Sugarhill that released two of the most important message raps of all time. Rap music had been growing in popularity for some time before it was brought to the attention of record company boss Sylvia Robinson. Legend has it she first saw a group of rappers performing at her son's birthday party, signed them to her label, christened them the Sugarhill Gang and helped pen their smash hit 'Rapper's Delight' (although the royalties were subsequently claimed by Chic).

The success of the Sugarhill Gang led to a plethora of rap acts being snapped up by both major and minor labels across the States, with Grandmaster Flash (real name Joseph Saddler) and the Furious Five signing first with Enjoy, Brass and Bozo Meko before signing with Sugarhill. This was undoubtedly their spiritual home and the group quickly became the first of rap's trailblazers.

Written by Sylvia Robinson and Melvyn Glover (Melle Mel), 'The Message', released in 1982, was one of the most important rap records of all time, a million-seller and a Top 10 R&B hit, although it failed to translate that success on to the pop charts. By the time 'White Lines

(Don't Don't Do It)' was released, the group had began to splinter into other units, with the single being credited to Grandmaster Flash and Melle Mel.

The anti-cocaine message was arguably negated by the admission from the singer that he participates himself – hence the double-negative in the song title. Dave Marsh, in his book *The Heart Of Rock And Soul*, points out the similarities between drug slang and music jargon: 'when the bass hits its stride,' he says, 'heralded by the cry "Free base!" the effect is a little like having a supersonic jet pass over your house.'

'White Lines' became a huge R&B and club hit. Its performance in the UK was little short of amazing: having initially spent only three weeks and peaked at Number 60 in November 1983, it re-entered the charts in February and hit Number 7. More importantly, it showed little sign of wanting to leave the charts, remaining listed for 38 weeks. It also returned on two further occasions, and was then remixed in 1994 and charted once again.

While Grandmaster Flash, the Furious Five and Melle Mel have yet to return to such heights, 'White Lines' was a monumental record, for music in general and rap in particular. Duran Duran tried covering it in 1995 and were rewarded with a hit, but the original remains rap's finest moment.

First released:	1983
Highest UK chart position:	7
Highest US chart position:	–

145

signs of the times

The Vietnam war led to hundreds of songs from American writers, but relatively few British writers wrote about the Falklands conflict, which, incidentally, was never officially declared a war. Nevertheless, the hostilities did result in one undeniably great song in 'Shipbuilding', written by Elvis Costello and record producer Clive Langer.

It began life as a piano melody written by ex-Deaf School musician Langer. He asked Elvis if he could write some lyrics that would suit one of his artists, Robert Wyatt – a former member of Soft Machine and Matching Mole. He had fallen from a window which had left him paralyzed and confined to a wheelchair. He still recorded, and as he was a committed Marxist he wasn't afraid of tackling sensitive issues. However, at the time there was no indication that Clive's melody should be anything more than a love song.

shipbuilding

elvis costello

The British Government had refused to cede the Falklands Islands to Argentina, and so they in turn occupied the country and assumed sovereignty. The Government retaliated and 300 Argentinian sailors drowned with the sinking of the *Belgrano*. *The Sun* newspaper, in gung-ho fashion, came up with its 'Gotcha!' headline. Elvis Costello was on tour in Australia and he found that the Australian press coverage was even more offensive. The conflict was in danger of escalating to a full-scale war.

Costello imagined that the redundant workers of the Cammell Laird, Harland and Wolff and Swan Hunter shipyards would be needed again. More soldiers would be needed too and Costello had the notion, 'Your sons will do… just as soon as these ships are ready.'

In the song, an unemployed worker balances his desire for the shipyards to reopen against his sorrow at the destruction the ships will cause. He asks mournfully, 'Is it worth it?', thus making 'Shipbuilding' a song about how difficult the choice can be. The song does not mention the Falklands conflict at all, does not comment on who is right and who is wrong, and condemns no one. Or does it? The song is subtle and profoundly political. As Costello writes, 'Within weeks, they'll be reopening the shipyard and notifying the next of kin.'

In keeping with his promise, Costello passed the song over to Robert Wyatt, who released it as a single. He performed it quietly and without sentiment. It went to Number 35 on the charts. Costello's own version, with an elegiac trumpet solo from the veteran jazz musician, Chet Baker, did not appear until his 1983 album 'Punch The Clock'.

It was just as well that Costello hadn't been more specific, as the song would have been banned by the BBC. While the conflict was on, even 'Don't Cry For Me, Argentina' was vetoed. Fortunately, the crisis ended and the conflict in Costello's song did not take place. As he says, 'It was always less of a protest song than a warning sign.'

'Shipbuilding', 'Pills And Soap' and 'Peace In Our Time' form a trilogy of the best political pop of the 1980s – and Elvis Costello wrote them all. In 1989, he railed against Mrs Thatcher in 'Tramp The Dirt Down'. Oh, and in 1984, Boy George and Culture Club went to Number 2 with 'The War Song' – sample lyric: 'War is stupid' – and that's about it really.

First released:	1983
Highest UK chart position:	–
Highest US chart position:	–

News reports in the autumn of 1984 were dominated by just one story: the famine sweeping across Africa in general and Ethiopia in particular. Nightly news bulletins, especially those broadcast by the BBC, showing in graphic detail the plight of the Ethiopians as they trudged for miles in search of food, touched the hearts of the watching nation. One person in particular, the Boomtown Rats' charismatic lead singer Bob Geldof, vowed to do something to alleviate their suffering.

At first his attempts were small-scale: collecting buckets around venues where the Boomtown Rats were playing raised some money, but not enough to have any great effect. So he decided something on an altogether grander scale was needed, and what better than a charity record? He made contact with Ultravox's Midge Ure and together they wrote 'Do They Know It's Christmas?'.

do they know it's christmas?

band aid

In truth, neither Ultravox nor the Boomtown Rats possessed the fan base which would make the single an almighty smash. So Bob reasoned that with his and Midge's contacts they could draft in all of the big-selling acts, making this a true collective effort. While Bob began making the phone calls that set Band Aid in motion, Midge concerned himself with laying down the backing track, over which, on 25 November, 36 artists would lay the vocals. Aside from being a who's who of British pop music at that time, the recording session at the SARM Studios in London's Notting Hill was notable for one vital ingredient: everyone got on with everyone else.

While this may seem an obvious statement to make, it has to be remembered that British pop music has always been a mixture of styles and that not all the rock acts got on with their pop counterparts. Geldof was aware of this and implored all those who attended 'to leave your egos outside the studio'. They took his words to heart, and so the previous rows between Paul Weller and Wham! for instance were all forgotten while 'Do They Know It's Christmas?' was being recorded.

'Do They Know It's Christmas?'

It was Bob Geldof's contention that no one should benefit from the single other than the Ethiopians; the studio provided the recording time free, the record company (Phonogram) pressed and distributed the single for free – indeed, everyone gave freely with the exception of the Government, which still insisted on receiving VAT on each sale.

The record was subsequently launched at an Ethiopian Benefit concert at the Royal Albert Hall, an event organized by the Save The Children Fund. Eight days later it had crashed into the charts at Number 1, where it would remain for five weeks. Bob Geldof was perhaps the record's best salesman; he bullied, cajoled and persuaded the public to buy the record, in many cases more than once, with the end result that the record sold over three million copies in the UK, making it the biggest-selling single ever.

As well as selling over seven million copies worldwide, it was also the inspiration for a number of similar recordings, especially USA For Africa's 'We Are The World', and subsequently led to a live extravaganza, Live Aid, in London and Philadelphia the following year. In 1989, producers Stock Aitken and Waterman assembled a new cast of vocalists, reflecting perhaps a change of popularity within the pop market, and put together a remake that featured Jason Donovan, Matt Goss, Kylie Minogue, Marti Pellow, Chris Rea, Cliff Richard, Sonia, Lisa Stansfield and the three members of Bananarama, the only artists to appear on both versions. This too entered the charts at Number 1, and by the time the Band Aid Trust was closed in 1992, a total of $114 million had been raised and 98 per cent of it used for relief and development projects (the remaining two per cent had covered administration).

'There can be other Band Aids; there must be others, in new times, in different ways,' Bob Geldof said at the time. 'I once said that we would be more powerful in memory than in reality. Now we are that memory.'

First released:	1984
Highest UK chart position:	1
Highest US chart position:	13

Standing tall among U2's many landmark songs is 'Sunday Bloody Sunday', even though it was never released as a single. Having made their name with two exuberant if somewhat unfocused albums, 'Boy' (1980) and 'October' (1981), the band would hit a new creative and commercial peak with 1983's 'War'. Having achieved their first UK chart-topper (and reached Number 12 in the States), they had then split with producer Steve Lillywhite, the man hitherto responsible for their bombastic sound, and linked with Brian Eno and Daniel Lanois for another, more subtle, take on radio-friendly hard rock.

sunday bloody sunday

U2

There had been stresses and strains on the way to the top for the four former school friends from Dublin – and singer Bono admitted that 'When we were making "War" we went practically to the brink of breaking up the band. When we go into the studio,' he continued, 'we draw totally on our deepest resources and stretch them to the limit. If a band is going to be honest they've got to bring out everything, even the things that might frighten them.'

This more adventurous approach came up with songs that addressed wider political issues, and 'Sunday Bloody Sunday', the opening cut, controversially took violence in Northern Ireland as its subject. The incident that titled the song had taken place in January 1972, when an initially peaceful civil rights march in Belfast had turned into a massacre after British paratroops fired on a faction of demonstrators who attempted to break down a roadblock. Thirteen had been killed and another seventeen injured in an incident that caused much resentment among the North's Catholic minority.

Bono, who had a Protestant father and a Catholic mother, didn't need telling what a grey area this was. 'There are no sides, and I think people know better now… I think we've contributed to that.' When the band first played the song live in October 1982, it was in the very city where the Bloody Sunday massacre had taken place. In an unprecedented move, they announced from the stage that they would never play it again if the Belfast audience didn't approve of it. 'Out of 3,000 in the hall, only about three walked out,' recalled guitarist the Edge.

Lyricist Bono, who admitted he had been influenced in his writing of the song by the early-1970s sloganeering of John Lennon, later revealed that his intention had been to contrast Easter Sunday and Bloody Sunday. 'A lot of those lyrics I'm very proud of, and I'm proud of them almost because they were written so quickly and so naively… But it's a big idea to take on.'

The band that in 1983 had arrived 'with a placard in our hands' would go through many different styles and images before topping the charts in 1997 with 'Discotheque', a single that ironically appeared to celebrate the kind of heads-in-the-sand attitude the singer had once decried. 'Some love songs devalue the meaning of the word,' he'd said then, while comparing his current album to its chart competition. 'Disco bands turn it into a cliché by tearing it down until it means nothing. The power of love is always more striking when set against realism than when set against escapism.'

On the other hand, you could hardly blame U2 for indulging in a little 'Pop' escapism: 14 years of 'War' would have been tough on the nerves. And, after a brief 18-month ceasefire, the Troubles continued, making the questioning chorus 'How long, how long must we sing this song?' an even more poignant one.

First released:	1983
Highest UK chart position:	–
Highest US chart position:	–

Having created a perfect pop song in 'Every Breath You Take', Sting disbanded the Police with a solo career in mind. Yet if the lighthearted calypso mood of 'Dream Of The Blue Turtles', his first solo effort, seemed deliberately at odds with his recent, more serious stance, the balance was redressed in 1987 with the release of 'Nothing Like The Sun'.

It was an album designed to take advantage of the new compact disc format, which could accommodate up to 80 minutes of music. The sheer length of 'They Dance Alone' – 7 minutes and 16 seconds – might have been considered excessive on a vinyl release of 20 minutes a side. And while the most-played track on the album in the subsequent decade would be the annoyingly jolly 'Englishman In New York', thanks to a Rover cars ad campaign, track five was far more indicative of where the former Police-man's head was at.

they dance alone
(gueca solo)

sting

Sting had appeared at Live Aid, usually remembered as the decade's main charity fund-raising rock event. But the following year, 1986, saw him on a mission to raise consciousness and prick consciences just as much as raise cash. 'A Conspiracy Of Hope' was a two-week tour in June that united such talents as U2, Peter Gabriel and Bryan Adams, with the intention of promoting the non-partisan charity's work throughout the world for prisoners of conscience.

As well as playing music, the acts on the tour were introduced to former political prisoners from all over the world, people who had been tortured and imprisoned without trial for their beliefs – and Sting admitted that the experience had touched him greatly. 'It's one thing to read about torture, but to speak to a victim brings you one step closer to reality.'

He was particularly affected by learning of the atrocities of the extreme right-wing Chilean Government under General Auguste Pinochet: imprisonment without trial and torture were commonplace in the South American country, while thousands of people had disappeared, thought to be the innocent victims of murder squads, security forces, the police or the army.

Ironically, the Police had experienced similar repression at first hand in 1980 when touring in neighbouring Argentina, where Andy Summers' efforts to stop a policeman beating up an over-enthusiastic fan by tapping him on the shoulder with his foot looked like causing an international incident. 'The promoter came over,' manager Miles Copeland recalls, 'and said my God they're going to put him in jail... who knows what's going to happen?'

In the end, ten minutes of post-gig diplomacy and grovelling saved the day – but it was a salutary reminder that even high-profile rock stars might sometimes be advised to toe the line rather than kick out at repression.

Sting hit back the best way he knew how – in song. 'The Gueca is a traditional Chilean courting dance,' he explained. 'The "Gueca Solo" or the dance alone is performed publicly by the wives, daughters and mothers of the "disappeared". Often they dance with pictures of their loved ones pinned to their clothes. It is a symbolic gesture of protest and grief in a country where democracy doesn't need to be defended as much as exercized.'

He continued to make use of his own privileged position to benefit others, opening 1988's Nelson Mandela 70th birthday bash at Wembley with 'If You Love Somebody Set Them Free'.

'They Dance Alone' was belatedly issued as a single in September that year as he toured with Springsteen, Tracy Chapman, Peter Gabriel and Youssou N'Dour under the Human Rights Now! banner, but, despite the presence of guest guitarists Eric Clapton and Mark Knopfler, it failed to make a chart impression. It was doubtless low on General Pinochet's hit-list, too, but perhaps that was the point...

First released:	1987
Highest UK chart position:	–
Highest US chart position:	–

signs of the times

AIDS was first identified in 1981, but it wasn't until 1993 that it became the subject of a mainstream Hollywood film. That thought-provoking big-screen epic was *Philadelphia*, although its director, Jonathan Demme, was quick to point out that the film was also about the American legal system and a range of other issues. Tom Hanks put in an Oscar-winning performance as the victimized gay lawyer, an opera lover (what a cliché), and the issues are sensitively handled, which is perhaps surprising from the director of *Silence Of The Lambs*. Affinity groups criticized the film for not showing physical homosexual love, but by taking this stance the film had a 12 certificate and could therefore be seen by all.

Demme has also worked with rock musicians, notably Talking Heads, and he wanted original songs for the soundtrack. A request reached Bruce Springsteen but he was not sure – he couldn't relate to the story and he had never written for a film before.

Jonathan Demme spoke to him direct and described Tom Hanks' character and the pervading atmosphere. In a complete turnaround, the singer was so fired up that he recorded a demo at his home studio before even seeing the film. Springsteen was a good choice as he specializes in story songs, admittedly usually of working-class life.

'Streets Of Philadelphia' has the feel of his bleak 'Nebraska' album and captures the thoughts of someone dying of AIDS, although the song does not mention the disease. Beginning with funereal drumbeats, the brooding, stately song is performed over the opening credits. Springsteen is especially good on the deterioration of his physical condition: 'Saw my reflection in a window, couldn't recognize my own face' and 'My clothes don't fit me no more'. There is also a live version where the crowd reactions are out of keeping with such delicate words.

Another new song, Neil Young's 'Philadelphia', was performed over the end credits. It played on Philadelphia being 'the city of brotherly love', matching Springsteen's song perfectly. They were ideal bookends for the film and both tracks were featured on the bestselling soundtrack CD, which also contained music from Sade, Peter Gabriel, Indigo Girls and the Spin Doctors.

streets of philadelphia

bruce springsteen

The sales of 'Streets Of Philadelphia' were helped by a video with Springsteen walking the streets of Philadelphia interspersed with film clips. The song was Springsteen's first US Top 10 single since 1988 and his most successful UK single ever. Both Springsteen and Neil Young were nominated for Oscars. Springsteen won, and the song also won four Grammys, including Song of the Year.

Springsteen said, 'Songwriting and film-making are both acts of faith, the belief that if you tell the story well enough, there will be some understanding where there was none before. I hope that this film, and in some smaller way the song, might take a chip out of the fear and intolerance and lack of compassion that we show for one another.'

First released:	1994
Highest UK chart position:	2
Highest US chart position:	9

cop killer

ice-t

The very first rap record to enjoy mass success, 'Rapper's Delight' by the Sugarhill Gang, had been a whimsical piece of pop. The lyrics meant nothing at all; the object of the record was to prove that you could fit ten minutes of words into a song designed to last three minutes. By the mid-1980s rap had moved on: songs now had to say something, usually with expletives, about the previous experiences of the rapper. Indeed, rap music had evolved into 'gangsta rap', with half a dozen acts leading the way – Ice Cube, Public Enemy, NWA (Niggaz With Attitude), Snoop Doggy Dogg and Ice-T.

The experiences of the three guys who made up the Sugarhill Gang (Michael 'Wonder Mike' Wright, Guy 'Master Gee' O'Brien and Henry 'Big Bank Hank' Jackson) and those who have taken rap to new heights couldn't be more different: when the Sugarhill Gang came to the UK for their only promotional visit, the first question on their lips was what was the age of sexual consent – it is difficult to imagine today's rappers giving the thought much time. Today's rap has a much tougher edge than rap of 15 years ago: the Sugarhill Gang rapped about Holiday Inns; their counterparts talk about the police and authority. The very nature of rap music is confrontational, but Ice-T's 'Cop Killer' raised the stakes. Any record that has the likes of George Bush, the Governor of New York, Charlton Heston and Dan Quayle speaking against it is guaranteed of notoriety, so was 'Cop Killer' worth it?

Three years earlier, NWA had released 'F—— Tha Police', a record that prompted the FBI to write to Priority Records (NWA's label) stating that they had taken an official position against the record. The group

were prevented from performing the number during their entire tour of that year, and it became obvious that no matter how honourable the intentions, the authorities were not interested in listening to black rage against the police. Ice-T's inspiration for 'Cop Killer' was equally honourable. 'Since 1986 47,000 accusations of police brutality were filed with the US Justice Department and only 60 of the attackers were prosecuted.'

But condemnation was just as swift. Time/Warner's board (Ice-T recorded for Sire, part of the Time/Warner group) demanded Ice-T be dropped and the record withdrawn; death threats were supposedly made against employees of the company (although it is hard to imagine who made them – the police, perhaps?); and a group of Texas police calling themselves CLEAT organized a national boycott of Time/Warner products.

Although the number of police actually killed by members of the public during the year went down by 20 per cent, Ice-T was unceremoniously dropped from the label. Indeed, 1992 was a bad year all round for rap, for Ice Cube's 'Death Certificate' was similarly banned across the country – the state of Oregon made it illegal to display Ice Cube's image in a record shop!

Ironically, the year of release found Ice-T playing an undercover policeman in the film *New Jack City*. As for the controversy, he was delighted. 'If you deal with music and you just bounce along the top surface then you're doin' pop music; but if you rock that boat in any fashion… then you're doin' rock'n'roll.' Two years later, he cited 'Cop Killer' as the music he would like played at his funeral.

First released:	1991
Highest UK chart position:	–
Highest US chart position:	–

signs of the times

The year 1995 was one of the most dramatic in British pop. Blur and Oasis released singles in a chart race to emulate the rivalry between the Beatles and the Stones, and Pulp, while not selling as many records, left them standing in terms of street cred. Their lead singer and songwriter, Jarvis Cocker, was on the wrong side of 30 but he had stolen the hearts, minds and wardrobes of many British teenagers. What's more, he had done it without losing critical acclaim.

Journalists from *Smash Hits* to *The Guardian* were madly enthusing over Pulp's 'perfect pop', and Cocker's pouting face and spindly frame, not too far removed from Jonathan King's, was everywhere. In 1996, when he interrupted Michael Jackson's act at the Brit Awards, he was seen as a man of the people railing against an egocentric American icon.

A poll on Radio 1 of DJs, journalists and pop pundits nominated 'Common People' as the Most Significant Single of the Decade So Far. 'A classic of its time and a classic for all times. Genius,' said *Melody Maker*. Okay, it didn't make Number 1, but that's only because of Robson and Jerome's 'Unchained Melody', which many regarded as the worst single of the year.

common people

pulp

In the early 1990s, most successful bands tended to be factory pop or inspired by the nihilism of American grunge. Suede, Saint Etienne and Blur were attempting a more natural, and inevitably more English, approach. With 'Common People', all they had been trying to do had been achieved by Pulp in one four-minute swoop. With its seductive cocktail of keyboards, violin trills, stampeding bass and a manic, escalating climax, Pulp had spawned a hit of truly epic proportions. Its sound was unprecedented but called to mind the pile-driving glamour of Roxy Music's 'Virginia Plain'.

It was Jarvis Cocker's biting lyrics that made 'Common People' such a contemporary classic – the song was about the vacuousness of the common people's lives ('Dance and drink and screw 'cos there's nothing else to do'). Hissing with vitriol and yet spun with warm humanity, Jarvis endowed his themes (class snobbery and sex) with wit. As *The Guardian* put it, 'There are always going to be records that transcend personal taste and achieve a kind of grand consensual splendour. "Common People" is one of those records.'

'Common People' was written in June 1994 because Jarvis sensed the glamour that was being associated with low-rent and low-life people. It was released before the rest of the album. Cocker said, 'I really felt that if you had a song that was in the right place at the right time, then you'd be an idiot to let that moment pass.' The theme of 'Common People' inspired Jarvis to complete the album, 'Different Class', which described differences between London and his hometown of Sheffield.

Pulp consolidated 'Common People's success with headlining performances at Glastonbury and the Leeds Heineken Festival. The set piece was 'Common People',

and crowds of 50,000 bellowed every syllable as though their lives depended upon it and copied Jarvis' kung-fu kicks like maniacs. Pulp had created a relevant and anthemic pop epic, another fanfare for the common man.

First released:	1995
Highest UK chart position:	2
Highest US chart position:	–

index

index